EVERY DEGREE DEBT FREE

HOW TO PAY FOR COLLEGE & GRADUATE SCHOOL WITHOUT LOANS

HOW I DID IT.
HOW ANY STUDENT CAN DO IT.
AND WHY IT'S WORTH IT.

JORDAN T. HALL, J.D.

Cover Art by Alex Weires Scott

ISBN 978-1-9858336-4-7 (paperback)

First edition, March 2018

CONTENTS

INTRODUCTION

THE FALL, THE CRISIS, AND THE EXPERIMENT

So, there I was,

A thirteen-year-old kid standing in my parents' bedroom listening to my mom. It was early December, nearing Christmas. Her room was a mess with bright and cheery wrapping paper and ribbon strewn across the bed, but her tone was solemn and serious. She was explaining to me that Christmas was going to be different this year. There would not be a plethora of gifts around the tree. My mind flashed back to the year before, recalling the abundance of presents I had received. "Jordan, you need to lower your expectations on gifts this year and understand that things will be different," she said. I knew what she was referencing.

In October, my dad had suffered an accident while attempting to perform some home repairs to our roof. He had plunged nearly 15 feet to the ground, landing on one leg. The jolt of the ground shot his right femur straight up into his hip, shattering most of that side of his pelvis. Now, two months later, he was still laid up in a chair in our living room with his leg in a cast. But that mishap didn't just result in a physical disaster for his body, it was wreaking havoc on our family finances as well.

Because he couldn't work, my dad—the sole breadwinner of our household—was on the verge of losing his job. However, unemployment meant more than just a loss of income. My dad was an eternal optimist and a serial entrepreneur. Over the previous year and a half, he had been putting together the largest deal of his life, developing a tract of land on the outskirts of our town with plans to construct a convenience store on the property. In order to purchase the land and begin development, he had entered into multiple loans, which amounted to several hundred thousand dollars in debt. The terms of these loans were dependent on his continued employment, and a job loss meant they would come due virtually immediately. This would spell disaster for my family, with a high likelihood of bankruptcy and foreclosure. As we sat talking in my parents' bedroom, my mom was keenly aware of the prospects.

She continued, "It's not only *this* Christmas that will be different. You need to understand that this is going to affect our family for a long time. We won't be able to buy you a car when you turn 16 or pay for your college in a few years. If you want these things, you are going to have to step up and pay for them yourself."

I sat listening, trying to internalize the gravity of this conversation as much as a thirteen-year-old boy could comprehend. At first, I was confused and worried. But then, I began to grow determined. Those words from my mom would have a lasting impact on me, but not in a negative way. The tough news she shared that night didn't break my spirit, it *made* my spirit. I think kids are a lot more resilient than most adults give them credit for. I was a boy, but my mom had spoken to me like a man. From that moment forward, if I wanted something, it was up to me. Beyond basic food and shelter, I knew I needed to take responsibility for expenses like eating out, gas money, and eventually college tuition.

In a way, I was being given a head start in life. I now had the opportunity to learn how to earn things for myself, well in advance of most American kids. That night my mom had spoken maturity into me. She had challenged me. I was intimidated, but also empowered.

My dad did lose his job. But fortunately, over a

long period of time, my parents managed to recover. Dad was forced to sell off the property he had purchased. As soon as his leg healed, he was out working any side jobs he could find to bring in money while searching for full-time employment. Mom was economizing at home, and the whole family was on a stripped-down budget. Many items were sold, and other sacrifices were made. Bankruptcy and foreclosure were avoided, but only by the narrowest of margins.

As my parents were beginning the process of getting our family's financial house back in order, I started researching ways I could pay for college and prepare for my own financial independence. I was ready and willing to work and earn my way through life, but I also wanted to learn how to avoid the pitfalls my parents had encountered. They had both been extremely hard-working and fiercely honest, yet they had not been able to avert financial disaster. I was determined to bypass that circumstance in *my* future. I began reading anything I could get my hands on about money. I devoured books by financial experts like Dave Ramsey and Robert Kioyosaki as well as Thomas Stanley's *Millionaire Next Door* series. I began to understand the dampening and potentially devastating effects of debt on personal finance. As a young teen, I vowed to never borrow a dime. Debt had wrecked my parents' finances, and I was bent on doing whatever it took to evade that monster. Even with challenges like a college education looming, I committed myself totally to this goal.

In this book, I outline my experience attempting to pay for college and a law degree without loans and without financial help from my parents. In the age of student loans, I wanted to find out whether it is still possible to go to school without debt. In the process, I learned a lot. I learned that it *is* still possible—for me and for any other student—to pursue education without debt. But most importantly, I learned that it is *worth it*.

The Current Crisis

It's no secret that the amount of student loan debt in this country is reaching crisis levels, both for individual borrowers and for the broader economy. At the time of this writing, the total outstanding student loan debt in America has ballooned to $1.48 trillion, with the average undergraduate borrower owing more than $37,000 and the median graduate school borrower more than $57,000.[1] The debt is growing so quickly that by the time you read this, those numbers will already be out of date. Despite droves of young graduates having their careers and financial lives stifled by ever-increasing loan balances, many people still characterize student loans as "good" debt, and some even allege that borrowing is the only option available for many students to finance a degree.

After spending seven years in the higher education system, it is my contention that education—at all levels and for all students—can and *should* be pursued without loans.

Student loan debt is insidious because it is easy to rationalize. Who is going to tell a kid they *shouldn't* do whatever it takes—and borrow as much as it takes—to get a degree? We have deified formal education, making it the be-all-end-all. The idea that a young person should *wait* to pursue college or graduate school or—worse yet— consider not attending college at all sounds like blasphemy to most people. We have overpromised a generation about the benefits of higher education and induced millions to borrow heavily against that promise. To make matters worse, we fail to warn young people that when they borrow using student loans the collateral is their future. These loans can't be discharged in bankruptcy and they don't go away until the borrower pays them off, becomes permanently disabled, or dies.

This system must be disrupted.

Is the Crisis the Crisis?

We live in a culture that is very good at identifying symptoms but not adept at addressing the root problems underlying those symptoms. I believe the student loan crisis isn't really the crisis at all. I submit that what many refer to as the "student loan crisis" is actually the symptom of several other areas of crisis we face.

A Crisis of Parenting

Today, out of some sorely misplaced sense of guilt, many parents who can't afford to pay for their kids' college education with cash tend to encourage them to take on student debt. This is unfortunate. Allow me right now, once and for all, to let parents off the hook: *You are not obligated to pay for your child's college or graduate school. You are obligated to provide them with food, shelter, love and guidance until the age of 18.* If you can afford to pay for their school, that's great. If not, that's great too. Your most important contribution to your offspring will be the lessons you taught them while under your roof—not the money you paid for someone else to impart knowledge to them. The ultimate goal of parenting should be to raise self-sufficient adults—not perpetually dependent adolescents. My parents could not afford to pay for my college or law school expenses, but before I left their home, they gave far greater gifts to me. They instilled in me a sense of confidence and independence and a conviction that I could accomplish difficult things. This has had a far greater return than any money they might have given me for tuition.

Our culture needs parents who challenge, not parents who coddle. We need parents who *expect* more and *protect* less. Parents without the backbones to tell their children "no" end up raising kids with skin too thin to succeed in the real world. The advent of financial products such as the Parent Plus Loan has spawned an epidemic of parents borrowing or cosigning for their offspring. Parents, kids don't need your money and they certainly don't need your credit. They need your wisdom. Those who seek to provide their kids with everything end up depriving them of the most important things like grit, determination, and self-confidence. It is parents who hold the keys to ending the student loan crisis.

A Crisis of Planning

Planning is the most important practical step to avoiding school debt. Debt is almost always the product of a lack of planning. Most students fail to take the time to select the most affordable school or program of study, to adequately assess all the costs associated with higher education, and to realistically tabulate all resources available to pay for school. Preparation is a primary weapon for debt avoidance, but far too many people are failing to prepare and are turning to student loans by default. Default mode is a poor life mode.

A Crisis of Hope

The main reason most students don't pursue a debt-free education is because the majority no longer believe it's possible. The news media, the schools, and other students and parents have resigned themselves to student loans as a way of life. The first step in paying cash for school is to believe that it can be done. Most students today don't believe they can do it, so they don't even try. But capitulating to the crowd early in life develops a harmful habit with some catastrophic consequences. This leads to the final area of crisis.

A Crisis of Conformity

In our society today, student loans embody conformity. We have a shortage of successful people in our world principally because we have a surplus of people who choose to conform rather than embrace the risks and rewards of standing out. Famous radio host Earl Nightingale once said, "People conform because they do not know where they are going, and they do not know why they are going there." For many today the path to financial conformity begins with student loans. Few students ever fully and adequately analyze whether they could pay for school out of pocket; they simply sign up for tens of thousands of dollars of debt because that's what all the other students do. It is very difficult to succeed at a high level in any life endeavor if we are unwilling to stand apart from the crowd. When it comes to financing higher education in America, the crowd is choosing student loans—and the crowd is losing. As Arnold Schwarzenegger said, "The worst thing I can be is the same as everybody else."

While mindless conformity carries many negative consequences, refusing to conform can have tremendous benefits. More than three out of four millionaires (76 percent) report that *learning to think differently from the crowd* while they were in their formative years was an important influence in becoming productive adults later in life.[2] With over 70 percent of students taking out student loans, choosing not to borrow for school is a prime opportunity to establish the ability to think *and act* differently than the crowd early in life.[3]

Questionable Advice

When I was in my late teens, I received from an older friend some advice I have never forgotten. The counsel was well-intentioned but in my opinion way off base.

At the time this friend of mine was about 40 with a wife and child. He had attended a prestigious college in the South and was very well-travelled. I also happened to know he enjoyed upscale dining and had a flair for the finer things in life. He told me, "Jordan, the best advice I have for you is to do as much as you can now while you're young. Get out and see the world. Travel around the U.S. and visit as many countries as you can. It's important to experience as much life as possible before you get saddled with things like mortgage payments, credit cards, and student loans. Live life to the fullest while you're young. That's what we did. And, man, I sure am glad, because with the debt load we have now, our life is really limited."

I appreciated the advice, but it struck me that this acquaintance of mine couldn't see the holes in his own logic. He wanted me to embrace the same short-sighted philosophy that had allowed his 20s to steal from the remaining decades of his life.

I'm afraid this philosophy is not unique to my friend. A majority of people in America appear to subscribe to this defeatist attitude. Our culture advocates a life model which advises to borrow heavily when we are young and then spend a lifetime paying back debts. I want to turn that paradigm on its head.

Super Dollars

Thanks to the effects of compound interest and the time value of money, every dollar earned before the age of 30 has the potential to be more than a hundred dollars by the time we retire. I refer to these as "Super Dollars." So, $10,000 invested could grow into $1 million, but $10,000 borrowed might mean we miss out on that million. Youth provides leverage. Good choices and bad choices are magnified when we are young. This is not to say that a few poor decisions in our 20s will be our complete undoing; it is merely to illustrate that our actions when we are young have tremendous power. They can produce exceptional benefit or incredible frustration.

Frontloading the American Dream

When it comes to sacrifice, I'm a "pull the Band-Aid off fast" kind of guy. I will trade short-term pain for long-term gain every time. Too many people in our culture use debt to delay sacrifice into the future, hoping to avoid pain in the long term. Ultimately, this strategy tends to produce one result: mediocrity. I am an advocate for massive action on the front end. The earlier and bigger we are willing to sacrifice, the larger and longer we get to enjoy the benefits. I am convinced that if we are willing to do in the beginning what most people *won't* do, for the rest of our lives we will be able to do what most people *can't* do.

The Experiment

I had decided I didn't want to do life my friend's way. I didn't want to spend my 20s acquiring stuff (degrees, cars, houses) and my 30s, 40s, and 50s paying back debt. I had seen the way debt had treated my parents and I wasn't a fan. I knew I wanted to pursue a college education and had even given thought to law school. However, I also knew that tuition costs were on the rise. It would be difficult to get through an undergraduate program without debt. I wasn't certain a debt-free law degree was even possible. I had already made the commitment though. Any education I pursued would be acquired without debt. If I had to borrow, I had to stop.

Lots of people told me I was crazy. "You can't get through school without student loans!" was uttered more times than I can recall. Most people didn't really think it could be done. I wondered if it could.

I decided to approach my education like an experiment. I wanted to separate myth from truth. Was it possible to get through college without loans? And even graduate school?

In the pages that follow you'll read about the conditions of my experiment. I had to do some crazy things to accomplish my goal. Sacrifices had to be made and pleasure had to be delayed; but in the end, the question behind my experiment was definitively answered in the affirmative. You *can* still get through college and even professional or graduate school without debt. I did it, many others have done it, and you can too. What's more, I'm going to show you exactly how to do it and, most importantly, why it's worth it.

What If I Already Have Student Loans?

Undoubtedly, many people who pick up this book will already have some amount of student loan debt. That's unfortunate but it's far from fatal. It's never too late to reverse bad habits. If you have more education left to pursue, the advice, stories, and strategies in this book could have hundreds of thousands of dollars' worth of impact for you.

A Note to Undergraduates

In the narrative portion of this book, I focus more on my debt-free law school journey than on my undergraduate experience. But the same principles apply in either case. Debt-free graduate school is just a bigger challenge.

I elaborate about my experience in law school for two reasons. First, graduate and professional school debt is fast becoming the biggest driver of the student loan crisis. It already accounts for the majority of the $1.48 trillion in outstanding student debt and is the fastest growing category.[4] It seems many students are abandoning sound reasoning and common sense when it comes to pursuing these advanced degrees. Secondly, while some may agree that a college education can be achieved without borrowing, virtually no one believes this about law or medical school, etc. I want students to understand that getting through all levels of education without debt is possible and is *worth it*. If it can be done at the graduate level, it can be done at the undergraduate level.

PART ONE

HOW I DID IT

I never let my schooling interfere with my education.

-Mark Twain

As I was beginning the first semester of my senior year of college, like many college seniors, I was still unsure of exactly what I wanted to do with my life after graduation. Thanks to some scholarships and a lot of hard work, I had managed to get through my collegiate career to that point debt-free. My options were open, but my future was unclear. I was strongly considering law school, but two major obstacles stood before me.

First, I had to get accepted. Getting into law school is a challenge by itself. Acceptance requires not only sufficient undergraduate grades, which fortunately I had maintained, but also a qualifying score on the LSAT (Law School Admissions Test). I still had several months to prepare and study for the test, so that part was within the realm of possibility. The second major obstacle, however, was much more intimidating.

Even if I managed to get accepted to school, how on earth was I going to pay for it? I counted it a success that I had made it almost four years paying for college out my own pocket, but those expenses had consumed just about every dollar I had managed to earn. At that point I think my checking account held a balance of somewhere around $5.65. I thought that sum might buy me the paper and ink to fashion a fake law degree. After a few minutes' deliberation, I even removed that option from the table. There were no easy answers.

I was pleased that I had chosen to work and sacrifice to remain debt-free through undergrad. My friends were shocked when I didn't join in the laments about how high their student loan balances were soaring. In fact, I usually wasn't around to hear the laments because I was generally off working. But still, I wrestled with

God's will for my life and whether attending law school without loans was a viable course of action. I believed my aversion to debt was both practical and in line with Biblical wisdom (see Proverbs), but law school would be the ultimate test of my faith in these principles. Perhaps a big goal like a legal education was an exception to the rule? I was determined to find out.

School Selection

Fortunately, there are few things that motivate me more than a strenuous challenge. I knew that a solid test score was vital, not only to bolster my chances for admission but also to increase the odds that I might be awarded some amount of scholarship or financial aid. I spent as much time as possible studying and preparing for several months in advance of the test.

Late in the fall I received my LSAT results. My score was satisfactory, likely sufficient to qualify me for most of the law schools I had been seriously considering. I wasn't going to be attending Harvard or Yale, but I would at least have a shot with most respectable schools in my region.

I had chosen to apply to three schools. All three were public, in-state institutions. I chose to limit my applications to these three schools for several reasons. To begin with, each application carried with it the required fee. While these are not generally exorbitant, to a broke college student such as myself, *any* fee was exorbitant. Secondly, my debt-free goal had greatly narrowed my list. In-state tuition is generally two to three times cheaper than going out of state. Likewise, public schools are virtually always cheaper than private—especially when it comes to law schools. So only public, in-state institutions were in my field of vision. Finally, I wanted to stay within at least a hundred-mile radius of home and felt that closer was even better. The reason for this was purely economic.

A few months after my dad's accident several months before, I had begun searching for ways I could make money. My two older brothers, who were in college at the time, had a handful of lawns they were responsible for mowing, and I was occasionally allowed to help. One day that spring, while my brothers were still away at school, I convinced my mom to let me hook our trailer to her van and drive me and our mower to a nearby neighborhood where several of those lawns were located. That afternoon I mowed five lawns by myself and made $135. To my 14-year-old mind that $135 might as well have been $135,000. I was hooked. Over the next couple years, I jumped headlong into the mowing business, quickly growing that handful of lawns into an enterprise that managed the lawn care of over 50 homes and businesses. This was my major source of income during college. In fact, I had chosen to attend Georgetown College for my undergraduate studies in large part because the campus was only 30 minutes from my hometown of Frankfort, where most of the lawns I mowed were located. I knew I would need to remain close by during law school if I wanted to keep that stream of income flowing.

In light of this, I decided to apply to the University of Kentucky (25 miles from home), The University of Louisville (50 miles from home), and Northern Kentucky University (90 miles from home). Early in the spring semester of my senior year, I stuffed my applications in the mail and sent them off, hoping for the best.

While I was awaiting the results of my law school applications I didn't want to sit idle. As a second-semester senior, I pretty much had my college classes on cruise control. I began to look toward saving up money for my first law school semester. Pending my admission, I would be starting school in August. That meant I had a little more than six months to prepare. It was February, which was usually my low point in income for the year. My lawn care business wouldn't be back in gear until April, and I had basically no other income until then. I had noticed a sign outside the local Domino's Pizza establishment that proclaimed, "Now Hiring Delivery Drivers." I had never worked in the foodservice business but thought the prospect of working for tips beat a low hourly-rate campus job all to pieces. I applied and went to work the next week.

I must admit my attitude with this job was not always the best. Peak hours for pizza delivery are late evenings and weekends. These are incidentally also the peak hours for fun on college campuses. Often, as I was leaving campus for work, I would overhear my friends discussing their recreational plans for the evening. Although I was frustrated and often jealous on the nights I couldn't join in, I knew I was making a sacrifice of my own free will that would pay great dividends down the road. There were many weekends I would work at Domino's Friday, Saturday, and Sunday nights, often until after close. If you've never worked in the restaurant business, and, more specifically, if you've never *closed* in the restaurant business, I recommend you give it a try. There are many lessons to be learned from scrubbing dishes in the back of a restaurant at 3 AM on a Friday night (technically Saturday morning). While I can't claim I knew what those lessons were then, looking back, that experience undoubtedly instilled in me a sense of humility and resolve. If I was going to be staying up until 3 AM scrubbing other people's dishes, it was going to be moving me toward my goals. It wasn't going to be for nothing. There were many instances later during my law school tenure when the studying would get tiresome and I would harken back in my mind to those late nights in Domino's. No matter how taxing school got, I wasn't going to let that kid who had scrubbed dishes in Domino's down. His efforts were not going to be in vain.

Fortunately, I was not relegated to working the pizza delivery circuit forever. By springtime the grass began to grow, and I energetically resumed my lawn care work. Mowing yards allowed me to make substantially more than just about any other job available to a college student. I began to work even more feverishly to pay off my last semester of undergrad and begin socking away whatever I could for law school. Virtually any moment I wasn't in class that spring, I was cutting grass. One lawn at a time, I was paying for my dream.

In April, I finally heard back from the schools to which I had applied. Thankfully, I had been accepted to all three. Shortly after getting my acceptance letters, I also received scholarship offers from each institution. The offers varied in amount, each covering a portion of tuition but not living expenses, books, or other fees. I was encouraged. I had known that it would be very difficult to work and pay ALL the expenses of school out of pocket. A little scholarship money would be a great help, but I would still have enormous amounts of cost to cover. The average law student at the time was leaving school with over $140,000 in debt.[5] Even if I took my best offer, I would still have to make up a difference of around

$100,000 to avoid that result for myself.

I need to stop for a moment here. I am sure you may be thinking, *Oh, well it's easy to see how he got through without debt, he had scholarships.* Of course, the scholarship money I received was of much help to me. However, you would be incorrect to assume that it's impossible to get through college or graduate school without significant scholarships. I will address this topic in-depth later, but for now, let me just say this: Whether you're intending to pay for an undergraduate, graduate, or professional education, doing so successfully without student loans almost always requires a *combination* of things. Some students will have the advantage of scholarship money and some won't, but each student will have his or her own set of strengths. Additionally, the vast majority of undergraduate students and even a sizeable majority of graduate students receive some amount of scholarship or grant money.[6,7] If you can get into a school, it is very likely you can qualify for some level of financial help.

The most potent strength I had in my battle against student debt was my mowing business. Mowing lawns may not seem like an impressive, sophisticated line of work and it's not. But it allowed me to work on my own schedule at a pay rate that maximized my return on effort. It was the perfect job for a student, and I took advantage.

As I will elaborate later in the book, school selection is one of the most critical choices to be made in the education cost equation. For me, staying within a geographical range that enabled me to keep my mowing business going was absolutely vital. Northern Kentucky University had offered me a scholarship which was significantly greater than the other two schools had offered. It might have seemed like the obvious choice. However, NKU is about 100 miles from Frankfort, and that distance would have made it extremely difficult to service my lawn care clientele. I knew that if I chose NKU, finding a comparable income source in an unfamiliar area would be difficult, and commuting that distance would be equally challenging. Ultimately, I decided to attend the University of Louisville. The scholarship they had offered was bigger than the offer from the University of Kentucky, and despite the fact that Louisville was nearly twice the distance from my home, it was still within a range that I could commute back and forth as needed. With the school decision made, I worked to finish up my final college semester and prepared to walk across the graduation stage and begin a summer of long, hard work days.

The Domino's Effect

I want to go back for a second and talk about my few months working at Domino's during my last semester of college. While I made some much-needed income, it didn't turn out to be the world's most lucrative job. However, I did learn some valuable lessons there, and most importantly, it was my tenure at Domino's that helped set my goals in stone.

I'm ashamed to admit that during most of my time at Domino's I was embarrassed for anyone to know I worked there. There's no way around it—I was arrogant. I don't know if you've ever noticed, but when you work at a pizza delivery establishment they make you wear a goofy shirt and hat and stick a lighted sign on top of your car, proclaiming to everyone as you drive around town that you are the pizza delivery guy (or girl). I remember thinking to myself: *What are you doing, Jordan? You are about to graduate with a college degree, have been accepted to multiple law schools, and here you are working a foodservice job. You're better than this.* What an arrogant punk I was. It illustrates my lack of security and self-confidence at the time, but whenever I had to deliver a pizza to the home of anyone I knew, I was embarrassed beyond belief. The worst moment for my ego, though, occurred late one Friday night when my then-girlfriend, who lived out of state, decided to surprise me. Since the Domino's where I was employed was located close to my parents' home, I would often stay at their house on work nights. That night I stumbled into my parent's house about 3 AM after a long shift, still wearing my greasy shirt and goofy hat. There, standing in the darkened kitchen, was my girlfriend, Meg. I was mortified. She had known I was working for Domino's, but I had been careful to never let her see me in my get-up. She was the girl I was trying to impress. I wanted her to think I was on the fast track to success as a future lawyer/entrepreneur. Instead, she was seeing me as I really was: a pizza delivery boy.

A Cold Slap in the Face

The other defining moment during my stint at Domino's occurred one windy Saturday evening in February. It was a busy time for our store, as were most Saturday nights. Counting on big tips, I had already been stiffed on several delivery runs, and I was extremely frustrated. Not only was I at work while all my buddies were soaking up the college life, but thanks to the lack of tips and the price of gas, my net take for the shift was negative. I was backsliding in more ways than one. As I was preparing to leave on yet another run, I began loading several pizzas into the back seat of my car. Because it was cold, I opened my front door, leaned in to get the engine running, and then opened the back door to secure the warm pies for their final journey. I didn't have a free hand, so I left the driver's door open. The moment I closed the back door and turned around to get into the driver's seat, the icy wind kicked up and sent the door turning on its hinges with the top corner of the cold metal door careening right into my face. For a moment I saw stars, but immediately thereafter the dull pain radiated through my forehead, nose, and cheek. When I finally came to and the pain began to subside, I was filled with anger. *Here I am doing what I don't want to be doing on a night I don't want to be doing it. It's cold, I'm not making any money, and now I am experiencing physical pain.* I sat in the car for several minutes and stewed. The pity party was in full swing. Then, the anger slowly began to morph into determination.

I realized I could allow this temporary moment of frustration to affect me in one of two ways. I could give up and take the easy way out. Everyone would understand if I let off the gas a little bit. After all, I had already been accepted to law school. What was I doing delivering pizzas anyway? If I just quit, I could keep my pride and go have some fun. Or, I could use this. I could turn that frustrating moment into ammunition for the dream. I decided that slap in the face was going to be motivation. It was going to be fuel. I realized that setbacks and challenges were going to occur even when I was doing all the right things. That's life, and there was nothing I could do to change it. The one thing I could control was how I was going to respond. That lesson would be immensely helpful down the line.

The Domino's experience also illustrates one more point. There is no place for arrogance when we are trying to accomplish something big. Arrogance might be the least productive character trait. Many times when I was wearing that stupid uniform, I felt I was too good for it. That wasn't true, and it also wasn't helpful. I figured out that if I was too good to do what it took to pursue my dreams, then my dreams were too good for me. Snobs don't accomplish goals because they aren't willing to do what it takes. They are too good for some tasks. So, if *you* want to succeed, banish arrogance from your mind. One way to do that is to throw on a greasy uniform for a few months. You'll also get free food.

Sarah's Shock

Just days before we graduated college, I recall many of my classmates having their eyes opened to the harsh truths of the real world. I vividly remember one girl, Sarah, marching into the dorm room where several of us were hanging out. She had a yellow piece of paper in her hand, protruding from a white envelope and a disheartened look on her face. "Well, here it is," she exclaimed. "I'm thirty thousand dollars in debt and I don't have a job." I remember thinking about that number as I glanced pensively around the messy dorm room. *Thirty thousand dollars*, I pondered to myself. *It's going to take forever to pay that kind of money back.* Little did I realize, that sum was pocket change compared to what some of the other guys in the room owed. And it was chump change compared to the amount many of my law school friends would owe three years later. The atmosphere in the room, which had temporarily switched to panic, transitioned back to light-hearted laughter when one of our buddies thankfully changed the subject. We all resumed the blissful state of ignorance reserved for seniors fast approaching college graduation, but in my head, I couldn't stop thinking about Sarah's situation.

For the first time, it hit me. I understood on a personal level that her student loans would affect every decision she would make from then on: from buying a car to choosing a job or deciding whether or not to attend graduate school. That relatively small amount of debt would have a big impact on her life. I had heard about the student loan epidemic, but this was the first time I had witnessed its effects up close. Those thoughts and the conversation in that dorm room stuck with me long after.

Graduation and Paying off Undergrad

On a sunny Saturday morning two days later, my classmates and I received our hard-fought pieces of paper. For me though, the degree was not as big a deal as the fact that I had managed to avoid borrowing any money for college. When I strolled into the student finance office to pay off the remainder of my semester balance, it was a moment of personal vindication. The lady who worked the desk had become a friend. She had also become used to receiving my mid-semester payments in rolls of wadded up cash and knew my stance on debt. The first time I had stepped into her office four years earlier, I had told her that I was planning to pay off my balance each semester, and she had attempted to persuade me to make use of the college's student finance program. After several minutes of spirited debate and facial expressions meant to communicate how crazy she thought I was, she finally capitulated. After the first several semesters, she realized I wasn't kidding. Now, as I was a graduating senior, she had become one of my biggest cheerleaders. The day I made my last payment, she came out from behind the desk and took a picture with me as I held up my final account statement reflecting a balance of $0.00. I had achieved my first degree debt free.

A much bigger goal lurked in the future.

Tiiiiimber!

I knew one of the largest expenses I would have to deal with outside of tuition would be housing. As I began researching options for where I would live in Louisville, I realized just how vast an array of accommodations and rents existed. Some apartments were outfitted for a king and came with a corresponding royal price tag. Others were cheap but complete rat holes.

During the summer before law school began, I stayed at my parents' home. I didn't mind that at all, but the drive from their house to the university was an hour on a good day and could double in bad traffic. I knew I needed an option closer to the school. I didn't need a big place, just somewhere I could crash after hard nights of work and study. I definitely didn't want to pay the $1000-per-month or more I had seen advertised for some rentals.

Several weeks before the first day of classes, my mom came across the classified ad section of a local newspaper. One of the ads was from a gentleman named

Steve who had a room available for rent in his large home in a nice part of town. He was asking $300 per month. I called Steve and set up an appointment to see the place.

My dad went with me to meet him and check out the situation. Steve's neighborhood was only about 20 minutes from the law school, but it was also on the east side of Louisville, closer to Frankfort. That meant it would be convenient for my many trips back and forth to mow. We turned off a main road and onto a long tree-lined street with attractive houses on each side. Steve's house was the very last one at the end of the street. It was a large two-story brick home with big trees and a pool in the back.

We knocked on the door, and when Steve appeared he was a slim guy in his early 60s. He explained that he was divorced, and the big house was more than he needed, so he was renting out the extra space. As he gave us the tour, it was obvious that this was a bachelor pad. The home was extremely nice but straight out of the 80s. The color scheme and decorations reminded me of the Fresh Prince of Bel Air. The room he offered to me was upstairs and had a small closet and a window that looked out the front. There was also an extremely small, extremely old TV mounted high into the wall opposite the bed. Steve assured me it still worked and had cable. Downstairs there was a nice kitchen in the back which he said I could have free run of to cook meals and store food in the fridge.

As Steve wrapped up the tour we began to negotiate terms. He asked how long I expected to stay, and I told him at least through May of the next year. He said that would work and that we could go month-to-month after that. Because I had never rented and never been to law school, we didn't sign a lease.

I thought the $300 rent was extremely reasonable but wanted to make sure I didn't pass up any opportunities. I told Steve I was in the lawn care business and asked if he had any work which needed done that could possibly offset rent. He immediately motioned us to the backyard. Behind the pool, running along the rear fence of the property, were seven tall pine trees. Steve said he had received a bid to have them removed for $1600, but if I was interested he'd give me the first five months rent-free for removing them. I didn't have a ton of tree-removal experience, but I knew this was a deal I couldn't pass up. For five months' rent I'd take the trees down with a hacksaw if I had to. We shook hands and solidified the bargain.

As we drove away from Steve's, I had a great sense of satisfaction. I now had my housing lined up and wouldn't have to pay rent for the entire first semester. Those trees weren't going to be easy to remove, but I'd figure it out one way or the other. I was ready for this.

With my housing settled, I prepared to begin my law school experience.

The First Semester

It certainly took some time to adjust to my new environment. Most law schools teach using the Socratic Method. This means that rather than lecturing in the traditional sense, the professors call on the students to answer questions and engage in discussion intended to spawn learning. Suffice it to say, you must be intimately familiar with any material which is fair game if you want to avoid looking like a moron. Merciless cold-calling is legendary in the law schools, and I have even heard tales of students being kicked out if they are found to be unprepared for class.

I will never forget my first day of law classes. We had been given our reading assignments several days before (pages and pages of legal text which none of us had any experience deciphering) and understood that any of it was fair game. We filed into the large, half-circle classroom early on a Monday morning and nervously chatted amongst ourselves as we waited for 9 AM. Precisely at nine, the professor walked through the doorway. He was young, probably 45, with a stern expression on his face. Without missing a beat, he marched straight to the podium, threw open his textbook, and demanded in a loud voice, "Mr. Collins, what are the facts of Regina v. Dudley and Stephens?" The murmuring which had filled the room at 8:59 instantly died away. The classroom was deathly silent and still. The Mr. Collins the professor referred to was Joshua Collins, a soft-spoken former high school teacher from Eastern Kentucky, mountain country. With quiet confidence Collins recited the factual happenings which had led to the case at hand. When he finished, he slowly looked up to see the professor's reaction. We all held our breath. "Very good," came the reply. "Now who can give me the rule of law we glean from this case?"

So it had begun. We all took a deep breath and dove headlong into our legal education.

The constant threat of being called on in class is one of the major motivations that keeps many law students studying. I know it was for me. The reading load in law school is probably one of the toughest things to adjust to. Often during the first semester, the pages of material we were tasked with reading each day numbered in the hundreds. After a long day of classes, I would come home and wonder how on earth I could possibly get through that amount of material. Reading quickly and efficiently became a vital skill. I was slow at first, but necessity forced me to develop this ability.

Throughout my first semester, I maintained working in the lawn business at my customary level: full time. I had 16 hours' worth of classes during the week, so as far as I was concerned, that meant I had room for at least 40 hours of money-making labor. I would attend my classes for the day and then immediately make the hour-long drive back to Frankfort where I would quickly assemble my gear and head out to mow as many yards as possible before dark.

Once night had fallen, I would haul my equipment back to my parents' house and get cleaned up. Depending on what time class was the next morning, I would either study for several hours and stay at my parents' house in Frankfort or drive back to Steve's in Louisville and get up early to study before class. It seems crazy now, but I really didn't think that much about it at the time. It was what I had to do.

Rules of Engagement

I also had another motivation that probably helped make the work less of a bother. Things were getting pretty serious with my college girlfriend, Meg. We had met in college, but she had graduated two years before I did. After graduating she had taken a job in the admissions department of a medical school in her hometown in

Tennessee and was pursuing her MBA at the same university. Somehow, amidst the working and studying we both had to do, we managed to spend most weekends together.

I had no doubt that she was the girl I wanted to marry. I hoped she felt the same about me. I had determined sometime after beginning my first semester at the law school that I wanted to propose to her before Christmas. There was only one problem—I didn't have a ring. I had emptied my bank account to pay off my final undergraduate bill back in May and had used most of the money I had accumulated working over the summer to pay for my initial tuition, books, and fees at the law school. I was flat broke, but I wasn't about to let a little detail like that discourage me. I knew I'd get the money for the ring, I just wasn't exactly certain how.

Toward the end of August, I began saving aggressively. I started throwing every spare dollar into the ring fund. It's amazing how work doesn't feel like work when you are working for something or someone you love. Those long, hot afternoons and evenings didn't bother me a bit. As I worked I would constantly be doing the math in my head, estimating how many yards I would need to mow to save enough for the ring I had picked out.

Tiiiiimber! (Revisited)

About that same time, I also had to figure out how I was going to take care of those pine trees for Steve. When we had negotiated the deal to exchange the trees for my first five months' rent, he hadn't given me a strict deadline, but I wanted to knock them out as quickly as possible.

Steve's trees were going to be a challenge to remove for two reasons: they were very tall and had several power lines running right through them. Rather than risk electrocution or a rerun of my dad's roof episode, I decided to enlist some help, at least to get the trees on the ground. Once a tree is on the ground, the job is only half over, of course. It still has to be loaded up and hauled off. I was confident I could do the hauling on my own once the trees were down. Fortunately, I knew some guys who specialized in tree removal. I asked them if I could pay them to help me for just a few hours one day, and they agreed.

One Sunday afternoon they met me in Steve's backyard. I told them if they could just get the part of the trees surrounding the electric power lines down, I could do the rest. One of the crew threw on a harness and immediately began working his way up the first tree, expertly using his mini chainsaw to lop off each limb in the perfect sequence to avoid getting tangled in the power lines or landing in Steve's pool. While the climber cut, the two others assisted me in stacking the shorn branches in piles. After about three hours, the foliage lay in Steve's yard in seven stacks each about the size of a car. Graciously, they even helped me drop the tree trunks and cut them up into short pieces. I thanked the group and handed them three one hundred-dollar bills. They piled into their rusty truck and took off.

Getting the trees on the ground was a huge accomplishment, but the lion's share of the work remained. Thankfully, I had a truck and a large trailer I could use to haul off the rest of the debris. Over the next several weeks, any time I had a few extra minutes I would bring my truck and trailer up from Frankfort to Louisville, stuff as much of the debris on my rig as possible, and drive it all back down the interstate the 60 miles to my dad's back field where it could be burned. In total it took twelve trips and who knows how much gas money. But for the price of $300 plus a lot of hard work, I had paid for my living quarters for a whole semester. That was a victory. I felt like a present-day Abe Lincoln, cutting down trees to pay for a legal education. The method was a bit antiquated, but the result was a modern miracle.

This little story about how I paid for my first semester's rent illustrates an important point for those looking to pay for their schooling. While some costs will vary, everyone in school requires a place to live. Housing is a huge expense that is virtually impossible to avoid. Fortunately, however, it is an expense which lends itself to creativity. You may not be able to pay for a full semester by cutting down trees (most people in this century can't), but you can work creative deals with landlords and/or fellow students to minimize this cost. During our college or graduate school years, we don't need luxurious accommodations. We need enough space to be able to study during the day and sleep at night. That's basically what a dorm room is. If a dorm room isn't available to you, I have found that rent is inversely proportional to the number of roommates you have. So find a rental house and get 68 roommates. If you can live with parents or grandparents on the cheap or for free, do it! This isn't forever. It's just until you get that degree. You can live in luxury after you have accomplished your more imminent educational goals.

The Proposal

Getting my rent situation out of the way freed me up to focus my financial resources on purchasing Meg's engagement ring. Several weeks after school had started, I began ring shopping. I talked with several jewelers in Louisville and even perused a couple pawn shops. In the end I decided to go with the jeweler which had been running ads on local radio ever since I was a little kid. To this day I can still recite those ads verbatim.

Meg's a very traditional girl and I knew she wanted a single-stone, round-cut diamond with a simple, classic gold band. This was fortunate because it allowed me to put most of my money toward the diamond as opposed to the band or setting. In truth I probably bought a more expensive ring than I should have. (Don't tell her that.) The saleslady talked me into a .97 carat stone, which I rounded up to be one full carat. (Don't mention *that* to her either.) During August, September, and the first several weeks of October I spent any spare time I could find accomplishing odd jobs for my mowing customers. If I wasn't borrowing money for school, I certainly wasn't going to borrow money for an engagement ring either. Also, I have always seen the idea of borrowing for an engagement ring as a little paradoxical. "Here is your ring. Now marry me so you can help me pay it off." I didn't want it that way.

Meg's favorite place on earth is Cades Cove in the Great Smoky Mountains, and her favorite time of year is fall. This made my location and timing decisions for the proposal easy. In addition to working full time and taking MBA classes, Meg had also taken advantage of the NCAA's new 5th-year transfer rule and had begun running college cross-country as a means of torturing herself daily.

She had been a four-year tennis player in college and wanted to stay active. As luck would have it, she had a cross-country meet near Cades Cove on the third Saturday in October.

The week before the meet, a friend and I snuck down to Smoky Mountains National Park and scouted out the proper location within Cades Cove for me to pop the question. We found a secluded spot with a great view and set about clearing out the undergrowth to make for the ideal picnic area. Somewhere in the brush I must have gotten into some poison ivy, because the next day my arms and legs were completely broken out. For weeks afterward I remember sitting at the desks in the law school library, struggling to focus on the law because the itching was so intense. I still remind Meg that the ring I bought didn't cost nearly as much as the price I paid for clearing out our spot.

When the day finally arrived, Meg ran in her cross-country meet in the morning, and afterward I nonchalantly suggested we make our way to Cades Cove. The plan went off without a hitch, and to my elation she accepted my proposal. Outside of the fact that I had to return to the law school on Monday, everything in the world was right. We set our wedding date for May of the next year. During the intervening time, she could focus on wedding planning, and I could focus on getting through 1L year. (In law school, each school year is denoted as 1L, 2L, or 3L. Don't ask me why.) The plan was perfect.

I include this story not only because it was an important point in my life and law school experience, but because proposals, engagements, weddings, and the like are common life occurrences for people in college and graduate school. School doesn't happen in a vacuum. Life doesn't pause just because we are trying to a get a degree. Everyone will have important life events that seem to distract from the goal at hand and which make completing and paying for school much more challenging. These milestones may hamper our resources, but that doesn't mean they have to thwart our goals. Nor do our educational and financial goals mean we need to delay life's most precious events. I wanted a debt-free education, and I didn't want to put the rest of my life on hold while I was getting it. It required many sacrifices; but in the end, they were all worth it. Undoubtedly, you will have similar life events come about during your own educational pursuits. Don't let them derail your plan and don't shortchange your life either. Within reason there's enough room for both.

While I had accomplished my most important goal of the year, the focus on planning for the engagement and working for the ring had caused me to partially neglect my studies. It's not that I hadn't studied. I had actually studied more than ever before in my life. I just hadn't studied as much as I should have, considering I was in law school. I didn't know that at the time though.

What girl could say "no" to this?

Post Engagement

After getting engaged, I picked up the studying a bit more but also kept working furiously. I now had semester two looking me square in the face, and I would need several thousand dollars set back to make my initial payment. I erred on the side of working more than studying.

One peculiar thing about most law school courses is they do not have midterms. There are no quizzes or mid-semester writing assignments. The entire course grade is determined by the final exam. During the semester, the student's job is to listen to the lectures, read the cases, and be studying along the way. This requires a high degree of discipline. The semester can lull students to sleep, and the final exams arrive abruptly.

That was certainly the case for my first semester. Before I knew it, Thanksgiving break had arrived. This is probably where I should have drawn the line. For the rest of my law school career, I knew to block off the last several weeks of the semester almost exclusively for study. But in my first semester I was still learning the ropes. I had been offered a job over Thanksgiving Break, assisting a local welder on a large outdoor welding project. He would pay me $15 an hour to basically be his gopher. My last class was the Monday before Thanksgiving, so I told him I could work with him Tuesday and Wednesday. That proved to be a poor decision. I ended up getting sick from working in the cold all day and, although I did collect a few precious dollars, the sickness wiped me out all of Thanksgiving Day and the day after. That meant no work and very little studying. My first final was the following Tuesday. I did manage to study most of the weekend and all of Monday. I hoped that would be sufficient.

The First Finals

I don't think many law school students ever forget their first round of final exams. I know I won't. The school was deathly quiet all week, and the tension throughout the building was palpable. There were tables outside each testing classroom that offered us students free snacks and earplugs. Earplugs are an essential component of the law school experience. Most law exams are taken on laptops, and the second the professor says "go" the noise of 75 students fiercely typing on their keyboards sounds like gunfire.

My first test was in Criminal Law. Most law school final exams last three hours. That may seem like a long period of time, but let me tell you, it flies by. The majority of exams are straight essay, meaning the professor may provide a prompt (what they call a fact pattern), and the student's job is to soundly analyze all legal facets of a given scenario. Before law school, I never would have believed I could write on any subject for three straight hours. By the end, three hours passed in an eye blink.

During the second weekend of finals, a local real estate agent for whom I'd previously worked called me and asked if I could take on a large leaf removal job, raking leaves out of flower beds and cleaning out the gutters of a house for winter. The job paid $400. I ditched studying for a large portion of the weekend and jumped on the gig. As cash-strapped as I was at the time, that $400 seemed like $40,000.

I managed to get through the second week of finals, spending most of my time in the library like a conscientious law student. The exams were extremely tough, but I gave them everything. I still had some major challenges just around the bend. The second semester was slated to begin the first week of January, and that was approaching fast. I would need several thousand dollars to make my initial payment, but the first semester school expenses and Meg's engagement ring had heavily depleted my funds. I wasn't panicked, but I was definitely concerned.

The Roof

In between exams I had also received a call from some family friends who were looking to get a roof put on their mother's house. They were aware that I had some experience doing construction work and wanted to know if I was interested in the job. I had no direct roofing experience, but I enthusiastically jumped at the chance. I mean, my goodness, YouTube was there to teach me anything I didn't know. What did I have to lose?

I explained to the couple that I had very little experience roofing but would love the chance to learn on the job. They trusted that I would do them right. I gave them a bid, and they accepted it.

The job would pay almost $7,000, but a large portion of that amount was cost of materials. I figured I could get several of my buddies who were out of school for Christmas break to assist, and after paying them and buying the materials I would net around $3,000. This sum, combined with the small amount I still had stashed away, would be sufficient to pay off the remaining balance on my first semester and grant me entrance back into the law school. I could pay off the balance of the spring semester when the weather warmed up.

So once again I had a plan. I just had to figure out how to put it successfully into action.

For the roof I enlisted the help of two of my friends who were in college at the time and eager to make some money. I also sought the advice of my neighbor Tommy. Tommy is one of those retired guys who knows how to do just about anything. He assured me that roofing wasn't very difficult, and he'd be willing to spend a couple days showing me the ropes.

With little experience but a lot of ambition, we set out to replace the roof. By this point it was late December and most days were freezing cold. We didn't have any safety equipment and I wasn't a lawyer yet, so I had no idea how many OSHA regulations we were most likely violating. We just worked.

Most professional roofing crews can tear off and completely replace an old roof in a day or two. It took us two weeks. Through snow, ice, and wind we slowly managed to get all the old shingles off and brand news ones on.

It was January before the job was completely finished, but after I paid off my buddies I did manage to clear about $3,000 for my trouble. I received the check just in time to pay off my bill from the previous semester and register for spring classes a few days in advance.

It was on that same afternoon that I finally decided to check my fall semester grades for the first time. The grades had been released for several days at this point, but I wasn't eager to look.

The Initial Grades

When I finally worked up the gumption to check, I was cautiously optimistic. I had made decent grades in college but knew the grading would be much more stringent in law school. I remember logging onto the university website after I had seen other students posting on Facebook about their grades. Everyone else seemed pleased with theirs, and I was praying for the same. I was hoping for a 3.0 but would be satisfied with something close to it. Because the only time I ever logged on was to check my grades, it was a struggle to remember my password. Fifteen minutes into the process I was finally ready for the big reveal.

There were my classes: Contracts, Criminal Law, Civil Procedure, Torts, and Legal Research. Before I could scan each class grade individually, my eyes instinctively dropped to the bottom row. The one displaying the cumulative GPA. It read:

Cumulative GPA: 1.666

I sat in stunned silence.

My initial thought was that I must be reading this wrong. After all, this system was new to me. I refreshed the page and reinitiated the process, selecting "check grades" and observing the website recalibrate. There it was again. Cumulative GPA: 1.666. This time I glanced up at the individual class grades. Reality began to sink in. I had made one B in Civil Procedure, but that was my best grade. I had managed C's in Criminal Law and Legal Research, but it appeared I had made D's in both Contracts and Torts.

Two D's? I had never made a D in a class in my life! I had only made one C in my entire college career.

Suddenly my mind began to race. What did this mean? I recalled that my scholarship letter had stipulated that my scholarship required that I maintain a 2.0 average. I had noticed that requirement months ago but never given it a moment's thought. Until now. I never thought that would be in question. *Does this mean I will lose my scholarship*? I immediately navigated to the law school's website and looked up the student handbook. It got worse. Not only did it appear that I would lose my scholarship, but less than a 2.0 grade point average placed me on academic probation. *Me, on academic probation.* If I couldn't raise my cumulative GPA above a 2.0 within the next semester, I would be asked to leave the school. I minimized the internet tab and bowed my head in shock.

I had not seen this coming. I had mentally prepared for lower grades but never dreamed I would be making D's. I had studied harder throughout that fall semester than I ever had before. I began to seriously question whether I should immediately drop out of school.

The next day I made the revelation to Meg. She couldn't believe it. Being the supportive fiancée that she was, she made some very kind, affirming comments, but I could tell she was legitimately surprised. Then I told my parents. I explained to them that their son whom they had loved and invested in was on track to be a law school failure. They were kind and encouraging like good parents ought to be. But neither they nor I could deny that this was not a good situation.

I would be lying if I said that I didn't sulk around for several days. Disappointment morphed into self-pity. I thought about all my law school comrades who I had seen posting gleefully on social media about their grades. Then

I started making excuses for myself. *None of them were working the long hours I was working during the semester. Heck, most of them didn't even have jobs. I'd like to see how they would wind up if they had been working like a dog.*

As the first day of classes for the spring semester approached, I had a big decision to make. I considered the prospect of quitting very seriously. I had tried and didn't make it. Debt-free law school might not be in the cards for me. I could take a semester off and regroup next year. If I borrowed just a little money to live on, I could devote more time to study and surely bring my grades up. Or I could abandon the law school dream altogether. After all, I didn't have any debt, so quitting wouldn't even leave me in bad shape financially. I could get a "real job" or continue developing my own business full time.

None of that left a good taste in my mouth. Don't get me wrong, I didn't see quitting as the ultimate failure. I know lots of people who have quit school and gone on to great success. But if I decided to quit, I wanted it to be on my terms. I didn't want to quit because I was afraid to fail or I hadn't given it my absolute best shot. Nor did I like the prospect of being forced out. Staying for one more semester meant big risk—the risk of trying and failing. I wasn't sure my ego or heart could take that kind of failure.

Shortly before the second semester began, I spoke with the dean of academics and she informed me that my scholarship would stay in place even while I was on probation. She also made another comment in our meeting that was very impactful. "Lots of people have come back from first-semester failure," she said. "It's just a matter of how badly you want it." That was all I needed to hear. If they could do it, I could do it or I would fail trying. It would not be for lack of effort.

The Plan

From the moment I walked out of that meeting, I began forming a plan in my mind. I would study like no one had ever studied before. Fortunately, I had a little money left over from the roof job—just enough that I could live extremely meagerly and not have to work much until at least March. I could spend January and February neck-deep in books. I set goals for how much I would study for each class. I wrote down detailed weekly plans for reading, studying, and outlining my courses. My first semester battle had been financial. This semester's battle would be academic.

It was the first week of January. The new year was a new start for me. I had to wipe the slate completely clean in my mind. This was going to be my year.

During the first week of classes, I met with every single professor from the semester before. Four out of the five classes from the first semester carried over to the second. I wanted to turn my mistakes from the first session into building blocks for the next. I sat in their offices and received the brutal feedback on my exams. Some of my mistakes were due to poor technique or format, but most were diagnosed as a lack of thorough knowledge of the material. This was not easy to hear, but it meant that there was real room for growth. The volume and quality of my study time was the largest obstacle which had held me back. So the factor over which I had the most control was also my best opportunity for improvement.

Here Comes a Comeback

I embarked on a brisk study regimen. I felt like Bradley Cooper in *Limitless* after he ingested the pill. I was focused and clear and knew exactly what I had to do. I began spending every Friday night in the library and every Saturday morning as well. An upbeat soundtrack played constantly in my head. If you know the song *Comeback Kid* by Brett Dennen, that was my jam. This was going to be my comeback. I started waking up early to study before classes, paying rapt attention to each lecture, and outlining thoroughly every afternoon. If there was a resource available which could potentially help improve my grades, I took advantage of it. The school began to take on an entirely different feel to me.

This time, I was emotionally invested. I didn't hold anything back. I also employed a strategy which I hadn't in the first semester. Meg and I had set our wedding date for the end of May, just a couple weeks after final exams. A Caribbean honeymoon would follow. I knew that these events would be fantastic no matter what, but they would feel a lot better if I was still *in* law school when they arrived. So I made them what I was working for. I wasn't worried about the next three years, I was worried about getting through the next three months successfully.

Day after day, morning after morning, and night after night, I slogged away at the books.

Toward the end of January, my meager supply of cash was wearing pretty thin. I had enough put back to pay Steve's $300 rent each month, but everything after that was a luxury. I indulged in a meal at my parents' house any time I could, but since they lived an hour away, that was not always readily available. Fortunately, one of my older brothers lived just a few miles away from Steve's house in another part of Louisville. I don't know whether it was out of pity or an honest need for cheap labor, but he offered to pay me by the hour to paint his living room and kitchen. While I was there, I could share in their meals as well. I jumped at the chance, as my rigorous study schedule had prevented me from taking advantage of many other income opportunities. It wasn't a ton, but those few dollars I earned were a huge boost to my morale. I even sprung for a Saturday lunch at Chili's with a portion of the proceeds.

As winter began to wane and the temperatures began to warm, my thoughts also turned to my summer plans. Many of my fellow law students were lining up internships with the various law firms around town. Some of these were paid, others were not. The students with the highest grades from the first semester earned the privilege of interviewing with the top local firms for the best paid internships. Obviously, I hadn't qualified for that list.

Instead of lawyering, I knew my top priority for the summer was going to be cutting as much grass as humanly possible. I could make more money mowing from sun up to sun down than I could at even the best law firm internship. I knew if I worked hard and supplemented my grass cutting with other odd jobs, I could accrue the necessary funds for my second year. I must admit I felt like I was falling behind when I saw most of the other students planning to spend their summer within a law firm. However, I reminded myself that a summer internship wasn't going to benefit my long-term career as much as graduating without debt. I was starting to get used to making decisions differently than most of my peers.

Spring break, which fell in the middle of March, was a welcome reprieve. I got caught up on some studying but also had time to work and make some money and get prepared for the upcoming mowing season.

When we returned from the break, it was easier to study, knowing that there weren't many weeks of the school year left. At this point, with the grass beginning to grow, I had to fend off temptations to hit the mowing trail any time I got tired of studying. I did a little outdoor work but recruited help to handle most of my yards, so I could focus on academics.

As the semester drew to its final weeks, doubt and worry began to creep in. I knew I had invested as much effort as possible in studying and preparing, but that only added to the worry. What if I really gave it my all and *still* failed? When these voices arose, I found the best way to silence them was to go right back to the books. Action dissipates anxiety. My goal was to give it my best shot and leave the results to God.

Two weeks before final exams were to begin, I threw myself completely into study mode. If I wasn't in class, I was studying. By this time Meg had a new job and had relocated from Tennessee to Louisville, renting an apartment which we would share as a married couple. I spent most of my time there. While she was at work, it provided a solitary, quiet study chamber. I would wake up and be over to hit the books by 7 AM at the latest. That allowed me to get in at least five hours of study by lunch time. After a brief lunch, I would resume my study for the remainder of the afternoon, maybe taking a short exercise break before dinner. After dinner I could usually knock out another several hours of study before retiring at about 10

PM. This was my life for the last couple weeks of the semester and into finals week. Unless I was in class or taking an exam, I was relentlessly studying my outlines.

Finally, the time for exams arrived. First Property Law (my favorite class), then Contract Law, followed by Torts and Civil Procedure the following week. The night before one exam, I had a solemn meal at an O'Charley's restaurant, eating alone with my note cards and study outline. I felt the gravity of these exams. The pressure was intense. If I didn't succeed this time, my whole plan was caput. I knew there was still plenty of opportunity for me even if I didn't remain in law school, but the prospect of failing would take a heavy mental toll. I tried not to think about that.

After two weeks of the grueling finals gauntlet, it was over at last. I strode out of my last exam and into the warm Kentucky sunshine at about noon on May 3rd. The law school at U of L is located right next to a large egg-shaped lawn. The university grounds crew was out mowing and trimming that day, and the smell of the fresh-cut grass was the aroma of my freedom. I wasn't certain of my academic fate, but I *was* certain that my nose wouldn't be found in a law book for several months. Summer break had arrived! The only question was whether my break from school would last three months or permanently.

I didn't waste any time getting to work. Everyone knows the stresses that come with pursuing a degree. I always found that the best stress reliever for me was to get outside and make some money. I left the law school that day and drove straight back to Frankfort and began cutting grass. I did take time that evening to celebrate with Meg and some of our friends. The realization that our wedding and honeymoon were just weeks away only multiplied the excitement.

Of course, the thought of my grades lurked constantly in my mind. For two weeks I put those anxious thoughts aside. I considered not looking at my grades until we were back from the honeymoon, but I couldn't do it. It was one week before our wedding when I again saw my classmates posting on social media that our semester grades were up. It was a rainy Saturday, and Meg and I were out running errands. We had stopped at my brother's house to visit with my nephews. Because I didn't yet have email on my phone, I asked if I could borrow his computer to check. He obliged, and I trudged down to the desktop in his den and pulled up the university website.

I recalled sitting in front of the computer screen five months before. Devastation flashed into my mind. This time I wasn't alone though; Meg stood right behind me. Wincing, I clicked the "check grades" button and waited for the screen to update. When the numbers came up, my eyes immediately dropped to the cumulative GPA column. I needed it to say, "two point something." If it was less than 2.0 my law school journey was over, and I'd be headed in a new direction.

But it wasn't over yet. I had upped my grades in every single class except one. My cumulative GPA had risen to the low 2's. Never in my life did I think I would be thankful for less than a B average, but that day I was ecstatic. To be honest, I had hoped to retain even better marks than I did, but getting off probation was what mattered most. With all that study, I was still toward the middle or bottom of my class. That was tough to stomach. Apparently, there were a lot of smart kids at that school who were also studying really hard. Nevertheless, I was still in school and still had no debt. Life was good, and the dream was alive!

Summertime...and the Living Is Easy (Sort of)

A week later I was married. It would have been the best day of my life anyway, but it was even better knowing that I still had my academic options open. We went to the Caribbean and had the time of our lives. Debt free, of course.

When we got back, it was time to resume work. The summer was my time to make up ground and save up money for the coming school year. Thankfully, I was no longer alone in this battle.

When people ask me how to get through school without debt, one of the first things I tell them is to marry for money. It doesn't have to be a lot of money. Every little bit helps! Meg had taken a job working for a small company in Louisville. She wasn't making a ton, but she was bringing in enough to cover most of our living expenses given our extremely frugal lifestyle. That freed up most of my income up to put toward school and related expenses. We lived in a small but clean and safe one-bedroom apartment on the east side of Louisville, convenient both to the school and my lawn customers back in Frankfort.

I hired a couple of buddies to help me part time with the lawn work as I had done during my summers in college. At this point we were managing about forty properties altogether. Later in the summer, I decided to expand our operation slightly. In the landscape business, I was constantly being asked if we offered any other types of home improvement work. One family, for whom I had been working for several years, asked if we would be interested in building a deck for them. I explained that I had just a little experience in construction but would be willing to learn more as needed on the job. They graciously assented, and like the roof replacement a few months before, I jumped at the opportunity.

Over two of the hottest weeks that summer, we stumbled through the stages of deck-building, learning as we worked. The process was especially slow because we had to take breaks to manage all the lawns we were responsible for, but eventually we got the whole thing assembled and our customers were pleased.

After paying for materials and compensating my help, I really hadn't netted much on that project, but adding home improvement tasks to our repertoire introduced a whole new line of work and potential income.

When summer drew to an end and school was set to resume, I entered the cooler months with a little more financial security. Not only had I worked hard enough that summer to cover most of the fall semester in advance, but I now knew that when the grass stopped growing I had an additional source of earning I could pursue.

Year Two

When school started back I continued working the lawn business through September and into October. It was good that the business tapered off toward late October because that was when the semester really kicked into high gear. Having adjusted to the study level of law school, I was able to make it through that third semester without any academic hiccups. I continued to study hard and collect sufficient grades.

As predicted, my newfound home improvement skills did come in handy during that winter. Over Christmas break and the first part of January, I remodeled a bathroom and a kitchen, laid some hardwood steps, and replaced three sets of kitchen countertops. The money I made from these jobs went straight to tuition and school expenses.

I cruised through the remainder of my second year, wrapped up my fourth set of final exams, and once again engaged in a summer of work. This time the business involved quite a few more home improvement projects mixed in with the lawn work. The summer was profitable, and as it concluded I faced what was set to be my final year of law school. It seemed the plan was working and there was very little risk of failure. It was all downhill from here.

At least, that's what I hoped.

Attorney at Lawn

It hadn't bothered me at the time, but when I was single and in school, I was generally living flat broke, continually teetering on the financial razor's edge. I would accumulate large sums in my bank account and then drain it every few months to pay for tuition and other school-related expenses. When we got married, Meg had the wisdom to make certain we always had a few extra dollars set aside for emergencies. This strategy would prove vital. In school, as in life, we need to be prepared for the unexpected to happen. That is why I advise college and graduate students to always maintain a modest emergency fund.

The finance office at the University of Louisville would not accept personal checks to pay for tuition. They *would* accept debit cards but added an additional 3% fee for this type of transaction. Therefore, I would always make my payments in cash. One afternoon, planning to make my payment at the school first thing the next morning, I withdrew $2,220 from my credit union in Frankfort. It was about 4 PM, and I still had several yards to mow before dark, so I stuffed the envelope of cash in my pocket and drove to my next lawn.

I zipped over the front yard on my zero-turn lawn mower and quickly moved on to the back. After making several swipes, I began backing up to maneuver around a bird bath. Suddenly, I heard a sound as if I had just mowed over a magazine or a thin phone book. It was odd. I hadn't noticed any trash or debris in the lawn beforehand. I always made certain to pick up any trash before starting each lawn. I slid my right hand into the hip pocket where I had placed the envelope of cash 30 minutes before. It wasn't there. Slowly, painfully, I turned my head to the right and looked down at the ground around the mower shoot. Fanned out in a half circle there were a thousand tiny pieces of paper colored a slightly lighter shade of green than the grass on which they rested. I paused for a moment, hoping I could rewind my life to ten seconds before. *Did I really just mow over more than $2,000?* I didn't know what else to do, so I immediately hopped off the mower and began frantically collecting the cash confetti.

I was at a loss as to how to proceed from there. Meg

was out of town on a business trip, and while half of me desperately wanted to call and disclose this mishap to her immediately, the other half of me was not particularly eager to confess my carelessness. I mean, how does one tell his wife that he has just literally run over thousands of their dollars with a lawn mower? So I drove straight to my parents' house to seek their comfort and advice. While they didn't know the exact protocol for salvaging mulched money, they spent the next several hours that evening meticulously piecing together each shredded bill. Their kitchen island was the backdrop for a thousand-piece puzzle. In the end, miraculously, every single fragment of the 24 individual bills (22 hundreds and 2 tens) was accounted for, except a small corner of one Benjamin Franklin. At that point, I called Meg. She took it relatively well.

The next day I went back to the credit union with the cash, which was now held together with clear tape. The branch manager told me they would have to send the money off to the Secret Service (the federal agency tasked with combatting counterfeiting), but there was no guarantee of receiving any of it back. She had never dealt with a case like this before. In the meantime, Meg's suggested emergency fund came in handy. We used most of the $2500 in that account to pay the school, which allowed me to continue attending classes. Without it my legal education would have been severely disrupted.

Luckily, several weeks later, the torn currency I had sent to the Secret Service was replaced with crisp, new bills. And the vital importance of maintaining an emergency fund was cemented into my mind. You just never know what might happen.

Year Three: The Final Round

While I had made it through two-thirds of law school, the final year still held some intimidating challenges for me. In addition to my regular classes, I still had to satisfy the law school's writing requirement. This would entail drafting a 25,000-word legal document. Writing has always intimidated me, but the prospect of penning a legal treatise of this length was particularly terrifying. On top of that, I knew my ultimate test—the bar exam—also lurked in the not-so-distant future. Despite these imminent challenges though, I had momentum on my side. I was excited to seize the school year and complete my education.

The first semester went swimmingly. I was able to keep up with my classes so well, in fact, that I decided to pursue yet another avenue which had long interested me. For years I had considered getting my real estate license. I had even spoken with multiple real estate brokers several times before about getting licensed but had never pulled the trigger. One day that fall, however, I once again began researching the idea and stumbled upon the realization that my law school classes would substitute for the 12-week course most real estate licensees were required to take. All I needed to do was pass the exam and I would be granted my license. I figured that if I could get my license and sell a few houses it would be another great learning experience and potentially a nice supplement to my income.

So I initiated the licensing process during the middle of the semester. The major hurdle was the licensing exam. I decided that I didn't want to interfere with my schooling any more than necessary and that I would take the exam only after I had completed my law finals for the semester. My plan was to schedule the test one week after my finals were over. I could keep my study momentum going and simply reapply it to real estate rather than law.

Another Set of Finals

My first exam was in Constitutional Law, slated for the first Monday in December. It was rumored to be one of the more manageable exams, but I didn't want to leave anything to chance. I put my nose back to the grindstone and marched forward.

On the day of the test, I arrived at the school as early as possible to make my final study preparations in the law library as was my custom. I glanced at my planner and then my phone to check the time. I had more than a half day to thoroughly review all my outlines and study tools before the 3 PM timeslot.

Just after 1 PM, I granted myself a slight reprieve to grab a small lunch and give my mind a quick break. I journeyed down to the basement of the law school to microwave a frozen meal and then returned to the computer lab where my books and notes were spread over three desktops. I noticed that the library had largely cleared out and I was grateful for the extra space during this final crunch time. A few short minutes later, I sat munching on my lunch, perusing through my notes. Just then my friend Bailey who worked in the library, walked into the computer lab.

"Why aren't you taking the Constitutional Law exam?" she asked.

"I am," I replied, "It's not until three."

Her face grew concerned, and it was evident that she did not want to cause panic, but it was also clear that she was not convinced. When her expression didn't change much after several seconds, I began to grow concerned as well.

"Let me check my planner," I said, my voice beginning to demonstrate obvious signs of stress.

I threw open my planner and quickly scanned to the current date.

"See," I said, pointing to where I had written down that my Constitutional Law exam was scheduled for 3 PM. She nodded kindly, hoping that I was right, but it was obvious she was still skeptical. I began to glance around the library, noticing that many of the students from my class, who had been present 45 minutes ago, were no longer there.

"Maybe I better double check the school website," I muttered.

Bailey nodded in enthusiastic agreement.

I furiously logged onto the school website and navigated my way to the published final exam schedule. There it was. Clear as day, the schedule read that the Constitutional Law I exam was being administered at *1 PM*. As I began to panic, I asked Bailey if she could look after my stuff, to which she readily agreed. I bounded out of the computer lab, through the library lobby, and down to the section of the school where the administration offices were located. I knew that the school's policy was to not offer any grace on exams. If you showed up late, you weren't generally granted any additional time. However, I hoped I might be able to be able to sweet talk the dean who was charged with overseeing the final exams.

To my relief she was in her office. I hastily explained my situation and related to her that even if I started immediately, I had less than two hours left to complete a three-hour exam. I used every tactic I could think of, stressing my innocence and communicating—almost begging—in an extremely humble manner.

"Unfortunately, there is nothing I can do," she frowned. "School policy dictates no exceptions."

I wanted to scream but knew that I had no other chance. I had to take the exam within the remaining time, which at this point was barely more than 90 minutes.

The dean hurriedly escorted me down to one of the overflow classrooms in which the test was being administered. She then retrieved a stack of bluebooks and a paper copy of the exam from the professor, handed them to me, and wished me good luck.

I sat for a moment, contemplating what had just happened. Due to my own incompetence, I was being forced to take the exam within half the allotted time and, to make matters worse, I was going to have to *handwrite it*. As I mentioned previously, most law school exams are in essay form, requiring a substantial amount of writing. Students are permitted to take these exams on their laptops with secure software provided by the school. However, it takes several minutes to set up and test the software before each exam. Because of my haste and the fact that I had left my laptop in the library, I was going to have to write this thing in blue books in my own hand. That would slow me down greatly, as I could write only half as fast as I could type.

All of this rushed through my head as I glanced at the clock on the wall. Time was ticking. I took a deep breath, picked up my pen, and opened the exam booklet.

That hour and a half felt like five minutes. I speed read the questions and wrote out my answers to each as fast as I could push the ball point across the paper. When the professor stuck her head into the classroom to call time, I was just putting the finishing touches on the final essay question. I folded up the several blue books I had filled and sheepishly handed them in as the rest of the class filed out of the room.

Ironically, as I left the law school and walked to my car, I felt pretty good about the exam. Despite my time shortage, I had managed to compose lengthy essays. Most importantly, I felt that I had answered the questions sufficiently to achieve a passing grade, maybe even an A or a B. All in all, I had dodged a bullet. If Bailey had not alerted me when she did, it was likely I would have missed the test altogether. For the remaining exams, I double-checked that each start time was recorded accurately in my planner to ensure this episode wouldn't be repeated. At last, it looked as if only one semester remained between me and graduation. The end was near.

Real Estate Exam

When my law school finals were concluded, I set about preparing for the real estate license exam. Despite the fact that this required even more study, it was a welcome break from studying the law. It had been a dream of mine for so long to get my real estate license that preparing for the test was almost fun.

I took the real estate exam the week after finals as I had planned, relying on a lot of the knowledge I had acquired in law school. Thankfully, I passed with flying colors. Now I was cleared to begin my foray into the real estate world. I could busy myself with this work while I waited to hear about the results of my law school exams.

The Worst Christmas Eve Ever

For some sadistic reason that December, the law school faculty thought it would be best to release the semester grades on Christmas Eve. I think checking grades is a nerve-racking experience for most law students, but given my experience from the first semester, it was always extremely emotionally taxing for me. Even though I was confident I had passed, a lump grew in my stomach when the day finally arrived.

As added frustration, the school leadership had disclosed which *day* the grades were to be released but never specified a *time*. This meant we were forced to wait in nervous anticipation, wondering when the determination of our academic fate would arrive. It was mental torture.

Since it was Christmas Eve, I spent the first part of the day scrambling to get Meg's Christmas presents in order. I was constructing a coffee table crafted from welded steel and barn wood. I had been out working on the project at my parents' house, because it would have been impossible to conceal this gift within our small apartment. By lunch time I had put the finishing touches on the table and returned to our place. Meg was still at work. Shortly after noon I noticed once again that some of my fellow students were posting on Facebook that the grades had been released.

As I had done so many times before, I trudged into my "office," the spare bedroom in which we kept a desk, and sat down at the computer. I recalled what it had felt like two years before to see my awful grades. *Thank goodness I no longer have to worry about that*, I comforted myself. I initiated the familiar routine through the law school website, finally reaching that fateful tab. As I gazed at the computer screen, I couldn't believe my eyes. While in every other class I had received a passing grade, the final row read:

Constitutional Law I
Grade: F

I had failed Constitutional Law.

I can't adequately describe the despair I felt in that moment. It had actually happened. I had officially failed a class. My mind began to spin as I internalized the consequences of this revelation. I wasn't going to be graduating in the spring as I had planned. I wouldn't have the privilege of walking across the stage with my friends, the people I had shared classes with for three years. Had I failed any of my other classes, that possibility would still be intact. But Constitutional Law I was a required credit and it was part of a tandem course. It was paired with Constitutional Law II, which would convene in January. Constitutional Law I was a prerequisite for Constitutional Law II. Constitutional Law I was only offered in the fall, Constitutional Law II only in the spring. That meant if I ever wanted to graduate, I would have to stick around for another entire year.

In my head at that moment, the dream was dead. I had hoped to prove to myself and to others that graduating from law school in three years and without debt was possible. But the letter grade said it all. Failure. I had tried, and I had failed.

One of the worst parts about this outcome was the fact that there was no good excuse or justification. This grade wasn't the result of me working too much. I couldn't whine to myself about not having adequate amounts of time to study. This failure was not the product of pursuing a debt-free education. It was the result of a single scheduling goof up.

I almost couldn't bear to share the news with Meg. I knew she was nearly as excited as I was to see this goal of ours come to fruition. She had already spoken to her parents about attending the graduation ceremony in May. I knew she was fervently looking forward to the time when I could have some relief from the strains of constant study and work and finally have a schedule freed up to spend more time with her. But that was going to be significantly delayed now, at minimum.

After sitting in disbelief for about 45 minutes, I finally got up the gumption to call her. She couldn't believe it. She didn't say she couldn't believe it just to be nice; she literally didn't believe it. "There must be some mistake!" she exclaimed. "I'm afraid not," I replied. "This is the real deal."

I didn't tell anyone else. I didn't know how to share this news. So many people were aware that I was in law school with the audacious goal of graduating debt free. Lots of people had said such encouraging things. Most of my friends knew I was getting really close to the end, but now I would have to admit that I had failed. So I just kept it to myself.

It was only December 24th, and classes would not resume until the first week of January. Meg wanted me to contact my professor. I knew that couldn't make any difference now, but I told her I would. In the meantime, I had two weeks to wait before I could get any answers or explanations.

We went to my family's annual Christmas Eve get-together that evening, but it didn't hold its usual cheeriness for me. I smiled and laughed with everyone but could not stop thinking about the disastrous news I had received. The next day, Christmas, we travelled to Tennessee to be with Meg's family for several days. I had looked forward to this trip for some time, but now it was a dismal blur.

I continued to wallow in my misery for the next two weeks. I think Meg began to worry. In general, I am a happy-go-lucky kind of guy. I have bad days sometimes, but it takes a lot to get me down and even more to keep my spirits low. I was down in the dumps continuously for fourteen days. I'm sure it was a real pain to live with me.

The Professor's Office

When we made it to the new year, my spirits began to rebound ever so slightly. I was still devastated that my dream was not going to work out as I had planned, but a little time had helped me deal with the frustration. Initially, I had claimed I would drop out of school altogether if I ever failed a class. I didn't want to be the guy who needed an extra semester or an extra year to get through. But Meg had convinced me that giving up was not the route which suited me. I could still accomplish what I had set out to do, it was just going to take a bit longer than I'd hoped.

As Meg suggested, I emailed my professor to try to get some answers. I needed to understand where I had come up short. Despite my lack of time, I felt so good about the test after taking it that it was difficult to imagine exactly where I had been deficient. She returned my email promptly and said she would be out of the office for the entire break but agreed to meet with me the day before classes were back in session.

On that day the sunny, hour-long drive to campus would have been pleasant had the gravity of the situation not weighed so heavily on my mind. When I arrived on campus, I trudged to the law building, climbed the stairs to the second floor, and then navigated the winding hallways to her office. Since classes hadn't yet started back, the place was mostly dead. I knocked on the door and she beckoned me to enter. I stepped into the office and immediately shut the door. I didn't want anyone catching wind of why I was there.

The professor sat behind her desk piled high with papers. She was flanked by a wall bearing several prestigious degrees, which bolstered her status as an academic elite. I took one of the chairs facing her. She knew why I was there but attempted to be cordial.

"How are you today, Mr. Hall?" she queried.

"I've been better," I smiled painfully. "I wanted to get feedback about where I came up short on my exam."

"Certainly," she replied. "Let's see what we can find out."

She shuffled through the tall stack of exams for several seconds before finally coming to mine. She examined a sheet of paper and then looked back at the pile of blue books. She repeated this twice more and looked puzzled. I began to question what was going on.

"Hmmm . . . ," she wondered out loud. "There seems to have been some sort of mistake."

"Mistake?" I perked up, straightening myself in my chair.

"Yes," she said. "Let me look again . . . yes, it appears that I somehow overlooked one of your blue books when I was doing the grading."

My heart began to beat at an erratic pace.

"You mean, my grade should have been *higher*?" I asked, trying to mask the urgency of hope in my voice.

"It looks that way, but let me run this again and double-check," she said cautiously.

I was on the edge of my seat as she punched more numbers into her calculator.

"I am so sorry. It looks like you passed after all. I hope I didn't ruin your break. I must have overlooked one of your blue books completely and not added that to your score. That was really silly of me. I will re-enter this grade and you are free to resume Constitutional Law II this semester."

She uttered this with a nonchalant expression, as if she had given me the incorrect change at a fast food drive-thru. I tried to remain calm as I shook her hand. I said something polite like, "We all make mistakes. No big deal," as I walked out of her office.

But it was a big deal.

By the time I hit the hallway, I was floating ten feet off the ground. Any anger or frustration I had with her mistake was overwhelmed by the understanding that the dream had been resuscitated. I was still alive academically! I burst through the doors of the law school and on to the lawn outside. I couldn't dial the numbers on my phone fast enough. After several rings, Meg picked up.

"She *did* make a mistake!" I exclaimed. "She somehow left out one of my blue books and assumed I didn't answer one of the main essay questions. I didn't fail after all!"

"I told you!" she retorted.

I could sense her elation through the phone. She had predicted there was a mistake, and she had been correct.

Of all the human emotions, relief has got to be one of the most welcome. It's great to get good news, but good news that cancels out bad news is doubly exhilarating. I could not believe it. All that depression and anxiety had been wasted. I was back in the hunt.

Making the Most of a Second Chance

This new academic life rejuvenated my spirit. I could now see the finish line. It was time to sprint to the tape. Fortunately, I was taking several classes that final semester which I really enjoyed. I had intentionally waited to enroll in the Real Estate Transactions and Real Estate Title courses until the end. I had such an interest in these subjects that I wanted to save the best for last. Now, the timing was working out perfectly as the material I learned in those classes was coinciding with my real estate work.

For the first and only time in my law school tenure, most of my classes met in the evening as opposed to the morning or afternoon. This was ideal as it allowed me to visit my real estate office for the first part of the day and engage in training my company offered there. In the afternoons I would remain in the privacy of my office to study and prepare for my classes and then drive to campus in the evenings. They were long days, but I was learning so much on so many fronts I didn't mind one bit.

I began to wish that I had started in real estate years before. It was going to take some time to really get moving, but I could already tell the flexibility of scheduling coupled with the income potential was ideal for my desired lifestyle. It had the added benefit of not leaving me covered in grass and reeking of gasoline at the end of the day.

During those first few months in real estate, I was fortunate to get plugged into a couple deals which allowed me to make a little money and learn a ton without interfering with my law school study regimen. I marveled at the opportunity that surrounded me. I was receiving a full-time professional classroom education while simultaneously gaining practical experience in a similar yet completely different industry. Each day I was gaining knowledge in the fields of law, sales, real estate, management, communication, and a host of others—and all without incurring any debt! The plan was coming together seamlessly.

Delaying the Bar Exam

The realities of life did force me to make one slight adjustment to my plan. I had always intended to be prepared to take the bar exam directly out of school. But as the final semester progressed, I realized that this was not going to be tenable. The bar was offered twice a year, once in July and once in February. Most of my classmates were planning to take the July exam, using the time immediately after graduation to prepare more thoroughly. I knew that would be tough for me because the months of May and June were typically my best months for making money. I needed that time. If it were a choice between studying for the bar or making money to eat, I would have to choose survival. I didn't want to add any additional stress to my last semester or take away precious resources. Graduation was my goal. Plus, the bar exam was expensive. It cost several hundred dollars for the exam fee and several thousand dollars for an intensive prep course. Delaying until February of the next year would allow me to work over the summer and save enough to pay for the bar exam fees and prep course and take several weeks off work to study for it. Since I wasn't intending to immediately join a firm, this wouldn't inhibit my short-term career goals. It wasn't what I had planned, but it seemed the most prudent course of action. If I could graduate debt free, I could then throw all my energy at the bar a few months later.

In the meantime, I focused on my classes and making as much income as possible. A March blizzard provided a cash windfall, as Meg and I spent my 25th birthday shoveling snow from sunup to sundown. Shortly thereafter spring returned, mowing resumed, and my last final exams were administered.

Graduation

When I officially received my grades for the last semester, I was blown away. I had managed my best GPA yet and even *booked* one of my real estate classes. In law school, "booking a class" means that you received the highest grade of any student in that class. I was ecstatic.

Graduation was extremely gratifying. My family helped me celebrate with a steak dinner atop a penthouse restaurant. I was on top of the world figuratively and literally. Despite many setbacks, the goal had been achieved.

All that hard work and money to get to wear a funny hat.

The Last Battle

It was done. I had conquered law school, earned my degree, married the love of my life, and managed to pay for the whole experience in cash. I couldn't fully celebrate this accomplishment though. A law degree is a wonderful thing to have, but it's not much good without a law *license*. If I wanted to get licensed, I would still have to face the ultimate legal challenge—the bar exam.

I had about seven months between graduation and the bar exam to prepare. Of course, I didn't study this entire time. I used the summer months to make money as I had planned. I delved deeper into the real estate world and continued to manage my other endeavors.

By the end of the year, I had saved up enough to pay all the exam fees and purchase the intensive bar study program. The course was seven weeks long and could be completed online. It consisted of video lectures and corresponding textbooks and workbooks. I officially ordered the program on New Year's Eve. Two days later a box with over sixty pounds of materials arrived. I leafed through them, observing thousands of practice questions, practice exams, and lecture notes. I was to work through *all* this material within the next seven weeks. If the law had intimidated me in school, it terrified me now.

The study program was designed to start slowly but quickly increase in volume and intensity. The first day only had me studying for two hours. It went up from there. Within a couple weeks of the exam, I would be studying 10-12 hours each day.

Fortunately, the first several weeks still allowed enough time for me to work during the day. I would wake up and study several hours in the early morning, head off to work during the late morning and afternoon, and then return to the books in the evening. By about week four or five, though, the intensity jumped into high gear. I would wake up and begin studying by about 6 AM and continue straight through until about 10 PM, only taking breaks to eat and exercise. It was extreme, but I didn't want to take any chances. I wanted to sit for the exam just one time.

Finally, the date of the exam arrived. The test, which was held at a large hotel in Lexington, was actually spread over two days with three-hour sessions in both morning and afternoon. It was administered in the hotel's grand ballroom with several hundred tables set up to accommodate all the potential lawyers. Typically, the prospect of travelling to spend a couple days in a hotel can be exciting, but this getaway was purely exhausting. After 48 hours of academic tribulation, it was over.

The Results

Over a month later, I was still waiting for the results. Fittingly, the moment that my test results arrived I happened to be mowing one of my lawns. It was just before noon on a Friday when the phone in my pocket buzzed, and I reached down to open the fateful email. I only read one word: *Congratulations*.

Ms. Donna Thompson's front yard on Breckinridge Lane will forever be my field of victory—my Yorktown. As I sat on that mower, the entirety of my three-year journey flooded through my mind. All the time, all the work, all the stress . . . was over. I was a licensed attorney. I was debt free. By the grace of God, it was done.

Life Without Student Loans

One doesn't begin reaping most of the benefits of a debt-free education until after the education is complete. That is one reason student loans can be so enticing. They make life easier while in school but much harder after. Paying for school with cash makes life harder while in school but much better after. I was ready to enjoy the benefits.

Hawaii

Three months after passing the bar, I found myself lying on a beach in Maui, Hawaii. It was a scene that I think well illustrates the rewards of life without debt. We had been able to take this trip only because of the fantastic position we had put ourselves in. Meg and I were only in our mid-20s and, honestly, we still weren't making a ton of money. Yet, we were experiencing a dream vacation most of our peers would not even be able to consider. What allowed us to be in a place like this? I think the reasons were several.

Most importantly, we didn't have any debt. This meant that our income was freed up to do exactly what we told it to do. I think people greatly underestimate how much further the dollar goes when it is not obligated to debt payments. It's great to be a doctor making $200k a year, but if that income is accompanied by $400k in student loans, its power is substantially limited. The money we made each month was ours to do with as we wished.

Because we didn't have any debt, that also made our careers much more flexible. I had elected not to follow the traditional law path and to pursue my own entrepreneurial endeavors, practicing law when and how I wanted to. I hadn't sold my soul to a firm to be working 80-hour weeks. Meg had been freed from her corporate captivity and was working with me. This career freedom allowed us to take life at our own pace. It also allowed us to capitalize on opportunities when they arose. Two of our friends were getting married and having a reception in Hawaii, and we wanted to go. We didn't have any debt, we had a little money, and we had the freedom.

So, we went.

PART TWO

WHY GRADUATING WITHOUT DEBT IS WORTH THE EFFORT

If you don't know your why you won't find your way.
If you do know your why you will make a way.

-Ken Costa

Don't Skip the Why

I have divided this book into three parts: Part One summarized how I got through school without debt. Part Two explains why I believe getting through school without debt is a worthwhile goal. And Part Three provides instruction on how I believe any student can get their degree without borrowing. The order of these sections is not an accident. I have intentionally placed the *why* section before the *how* section. I encourage you to read the *why* section and not to skip it, because you will need to remember the *why* when applying the *how*. Understanding the *why* will motivate the *how*. Think about the benefits and the success stories but also remember the costs, the risks, and those people who have been held back by their student loans.

I am well aware that what I am proposing with this book is not considered by many to be a viable route for attaining higher education today. I have an uphill battle in convincing you to try things my way, and you will have an uphill battle if you indeed attempt this feat. Chances are you won't be willing to do what it takes unless you understand and buy into the *why*. But if you believe the *why*, you probably won't even need me to tell you *how*. You will figure that out on your own.

Maybe you want to ensure career freedom after graduation. Maybe you want to be financially successful and you understand that graduating without debt is the shortest path to building wealth (it is, by the way). Maybe you are like me and have witnessed the havoc which debt can wreak in the lives of individuals and families. Whatever your reason—your *why*—you need to identify it.

If you don't have a *why* you won't get it done.

I'm going to help. In this section of the book, I am going to lay out the reasons I believe graduating without debt is a worthwhile goal. Some are obvious, others are subtle, but all are important. As you read this section, think about people you know who have dealt with or are dealing with the effects of enormous student loan balances. Think about the crop of young people coming out of school in the next few years and ponder how a new approach to student finance may change the destiny of a generation of graduates. Perhaps you may even be one of them.

What You Can Do with a Debt-Free Degree

In Part Three of this book, I profile several people who have achieved professional level degrees without debt. I will explain in detail the strategies they used to graduate debt free, but in the meantime, it is worthwhile to take a glance at how they are doing now to illustrate some of the benefits of debt freedom.

Taking Advantage of Opportunities

Getting through school without debt puts the graduate in the best possible position to take advantage of opportunities when they arise. I will talk more about how he did it later, but my friend Nathan managed to get through dental school completely debt free. As a result, shortly after he got out, he was able to jump on an extremely lucrative opportunity. Dentists generally make really good money, but dentists who own their practice have an even higher income ceiling. However, with massive dental school debt loads, most young dentists can't even think about acquiring their own shop. Because he didn't have student loans, Nathan was able to leverage his degree and catapult his career forward. He got a job right out of school working with an established dentist in his home town. Shortly after Nathan joined the practice, his boss decided she was ready to retire. Nathan was the prime candidate to take over. With no school debt, he had the financial resources to work a deal to buy the practice outright. Today, he has a thriving practice which has made him extremely prosperous. His opportunity-readiness was a direct result of his debt freedom.

Building Wealth

Graduating without debt puts the graduate on the fast track to financial prosperity. My friend Ben is a prime example of this. He graduated with a PhD in the sciences at age 26 and quickly secured a job in his field. Shortly after getting married, he and his wife saved up a strong down payment and purchased a home. Because they no longer had any other debt, they were able to make double and triple payments toward their home loan. At just 33 years of age, they paid off their mortgage completely. Now, with a paid-for home, no debt, and a healthy income, they are rapidly approaching millionaire status and will likely reach it before they turn 40. That is the financial power of a debt-free education.

Living the Calling

There's nothing worse than borrowing heavily for a

degree, only to decide after graduation that you do not want to work in that field. This is happening to a lot of people today. But graduating without debt provides much more freedom to pursue careers and callings outside of your degree field. My wife Meg graduated with her MBA and spent two years working in the corporate world while I was finishing up law school. Shortly after I graduated, she left her marketing position to come work with me. A year later when our daughter was born, Meg was able to fulfill her lifelong dream of being a stay-at-home mom— no questions asked. She didn't have any lingering debts keeping her chained to her career. She had put herself in a position to do parenthood on her own terms. Today, she couldn't be happier.

Pursuing Passions

It's rare to know exactly what you want to do with your life, even during college or graduate school. Most people, including professionals, don't end up working directly in their degree field during their entire working lifetime. This can be a problem which student loans exacerbate. But career ADD doesn't have to be a bad thing. I am an example of this phenomenon. As you know, I used my time in law school to explore several different career options. By the time I graduated, I had discovered a real passion and love for both home remodeling and real estate sales. Even when I became a licensed attorney, I didn't want to give up those passions. And thanks to our debt freedom, I didn't have to. After graduation I continued to grow both endeavors while also practicing law. It gives me great fulfillment to be able to pursue enterprises that interest me and offer attractive financial returns. My debt freedom has allowed me to continue to pursue my passions.

My Why

I have already explained a little bit about *my why*. I witnessed the stress and heartache debt had placed on my family growing up. My parents were honest, hardworking people, but had suffered a lot because of money. I didn't want any part of that. There was another reason why I refused to borrow for school though. During my teenage quest to learn how money worked, I stumbled upon one of the most beautiful and inspiring sights known to man: a compound interest table. Ok, that may sound a little geeky, but let me explain. For the first time, I saw how small amounts of money invested over time could grow into enormous sums, especially if a person started investing at the beginning of his or her working lifetime. I came to understand the incredible value and importance of having money available to consistently invest. I also realized that debt was the primary enemy that could prevent this from happening.

The Millionaires that Might Have Been

There's no reason the average college graduate in America shouldn't become a millionaire. Don't believe me? Let's look at the numbers.

The average monthly student loan payment in America was recently found to be $351.[8] The average length of payoff time is 21 years.[9] This means the average student loan borrower pays back $88,452. Remember, however, that the average student left school with only a $37,000 loan balance. In other words, thanks to interest and fees, most student borrowers end up paying back more than DOUBLE their original loan amount. That is tragic, but it gets worse.

What would have happened, if rather than sending all this money (most of which was interest) back to Sallie Mae, the average graduate instead had those funds available to invest? $351 per month invested over 252 months (21 years) at 12 percent interest grows to **$366,095.36**. But wait, there's more. If that money was left alone for just 9 more years without adding anything to it, in that short time it would have grown to **$1,081,421.60**. Wow. That means the average college graduate could be a millionaire right around their 50th birthday. The numbers are even more drastic for graduate and professional school students.

So why isn't this happening for more people? You know the answer. That money isn't available to be invested because it is already devoted to debt payments. It appears that student loans are the culprit that is denying a generation of Americans financial success, possibly even millionaire status. The truth is most college and graduate degree holders end up with above average lifestyles but not the level of success and opportunities that could have been theirs.

Why We Aren't as Wealthy as We Should Be

In his landmark studies of America's millionaire population, Dr. Thomas Stanley uncovered the secrets as to how these people accumulated massive amounts of money in one lifetime. He published his findings in a series of best-selling books, starting with *The Millionaire Next Door*.

Several decades of studying and writing about the wealthy made Stanley the preeminent authority on the topic of American millionaires. He knew a thing or two about how wealth is built in America and why most people never achieve financial success. His quotes are very telling about the contrasting financial habits of wealthy Americans and those who aren't wealthy. Consider these excerpts from his work:

"You cannot enjoy life if you are *addicted to consumption* and the *use of credit*."[10]

"Wealth is more often the result of hard work, perseverance, planning, and most of all, *self-discipline*."[11]

"Most Millionaire Next Door types are *contrarians*. They think and act differently. They are *savers and investors in a population of hyper consumers*."[12]

Stanley's exhaustive research ultimately yielded what he called the fundamental rule of wealth building:

Whatever your income, always live below your means.[13]

Borrowing money—even for school—is the definition of not living below your means.

Dr. Stanley identified that those who achieved wealth did so because they learned that borrowing money was not the path to prosperity. In fact, most of the millionaires profiled in *The Millionaire Next Door* admitted that it wasn't until they kicked the borrowing habit that their climb up the financial ladder really took off.

In a later book entitled *Stop Acting Rich*, Stanley contrasted the thrifty habits of America's millionaires with the hyper-consumption lifestyles of those he termed *aspirationals*—individuals who borrow and consume at levels far above their means and are more concerned with *looking* rich than actually *being* rich. The aspirationals represent a growing segment of our society stuck in the borrow-and-consume cycle, unlikely to ever get out.

Which type of individual is our current system of higher education minting?

Most graduates in America are being set on a course of borrowing before their professional lives have even begun. Therefore, it is no wonder that most Americans are not ultimately following Dr. Stanley's advice and becoming financially independent. Their fate is nearly sealed from the day they walk across the graduation stage. The financial habits begun during school tend to linger for decades after graduation. Most never break them.

College graduates earn significantly more money on average than non-graduates. Advanced degree holders earn even more. Conventional wisdom would suggest that the more educated someone is, the better they should be at accumulating wealth. But this is often not the case. There is a curious paradox when it comes to highly educated, high income earners: typically, the more they earn, the more they borrow. Debt tends to rise with income. Advanced education and increased earning often lead to increased lifestyle but not a higher net worth.

If we want to change the culture of America from one of borrow-and-spend to save-and-invest, we need to start by encouraging students not to develop the borrowing habit in the first place. It all begins with education.

Inaccurate Assumptions

All borrowing is based on assumptions. Students borrow for school based on the assumptions of future income and future financial prosperity. They think they will be able to repay their loans with ease later. And they don't anticipate anything bad happening in the meantime. For many, however, these assumptions are proving faulty. Students at all levels are borrowing based on a set of assumptions and expectations—many of which are simply not accurate.

The data shows that prospective students have extremely optimistic expectations about how much money they will make when they get out of college or graduate school and correspondingly rosy projections for how fast they will be able to pay off their student loans. They don't intend to remain in student debt for decades; they intend to pay off their loans and move on with life quickly after graduation. But reality stings when these former students enter the real world and discover that the high incomes they had hoped for are not always readily available, especially fresh out of school. It takes longer than they expected to reach peak income levels, and most start lower on the totem pole than they anticipated. Even doctors and lawyers are generally required to endure several years of residency or grunt work as a junior associate before they begin to make the big bucks.

In her book, *Generation Me*, author Jean Twenge highlights the disparity between the expectations of young people and the realities they ultimately confront. She cites a 2011 survey of 16 to 18-year-olds which found that this group *expected* that their starting salary would be $73,000, which they assumed would rise to $150,000 once they were established in their career. However, as Twenge points out, the median *household* income for all adults in the U.S. two years before was only $50,000, about one-third of the teens' aspirations.[14]

Most students don't progress through school as quickly as they originally expect either. Twenge mentions that in 2012, 84% of incoming freshman college students in the United States *expected* to graduate in four years, but only 41% of the students at their universities successfully accomplish this feat.[15]

Incorrect assumptions about student loans can have large, unforeseen consequences for the future. Unfortunately, by the time we, the graduates, come to terms with reality, our unmet expectations can be having an impact far beyond finances.

The hard truth is that loans made on assumptions are risky. Student loans are particularly risky because they are made to young people whose assumptions and expectations are often not in line with the facts.

The "I'll Pay Them Off Really Fast!" Myth

Most student borrowers believe they will pay off their loans rapidly after graduation. "Just get through school," they tell themselves, "then we'll be making plenty of money to pay off our loans without pain." But graduates are not paying off their student loans with any measure of quickness—not even the high-income earning professionals.

Take for example Florida Senator and 2016 Presidential hopeful, Marco Rubio. Few people have been more successful and made more money early in life than this man. Rubio, who graduated from the Miami University School of Law in 1996, made big news in 2012 when he announced in a speech that he had racked up almost $150,000 in student loan debt by the time he walked across the stage.[16] What's more, in that same 2012 speech, Rubio admitted that he was only able to pay off that debt after he received the proceeds from his first major book deal, *An American Son,* one year earlier.

Now let's think about this. Rubio graduated with his law degree in 1996 and began practicing. That same year he became a city commissioner of Miami, and by the year 2000, he was elected to the Florida House of Representatives. We also know he became a U.S. Senator in 2010. As a Senator, he was making a $174,000 annual salary. That's substantially more than most professionals will ever make, let alone before the age of 40. Yet despite all this success, Rubio still did not manage to pay back his loans until he received a major book contract. This should give pause to anyone who is planning to go to professional school and borrow heavily, expecting to quickly pay off their loans with their professional-level income. It simply is not that easy, even at the top.

Rubio himself has acknowledged that due to their high debt levels, his family often struggled to make their monthly payments, even amidst his unprecedented political career achievements. What could explain this? Is this family somehow unique? No. The Rubios are merely a highly visible example of what is occurring in most well-educated households all over America. Large debt balances—particularly education debt—are driving much of the decisions these families are making, and most don't have a congressional-level salary and blockbuster book deal coming to bail them out. They will have to pay back their debts the old-fashioned way—one demoralizing payment at a time.

As I said before, most students don't enter college or graduate school planning to carry their loans for decades into the future. They intend to pay them off sooner rather than later. Therein lies the rub. The hard fact is that most graduates aren't paying back their student loans half as fast as they expected when they took them out; and the existence of these debts is forcing them to borrow greater amounts in other areas.

According to a 2014 article by U.S. News and World Report, the average bachelor's degree holder takes 21 years to pay back his or her student loans. 21 *years*! Worse yet, the article cites a disturbing survey of current college students between the ages of 18-24. According to the survey, this group *expected* to pay off their loans by the time they were 33 years old, roughly 10 years after they graduate. In other words, the average college student expects to pay off their loans in about 10 years, but it actually takes them more than 20.

What about graduate students? It's even worse for them. The same survey found that the average length of time to repay graduate school loans was *23* years![17] If the survey was accurate, thanks to his book deal, Marco Rubio was eight years ahead of the average in paying off his law school loans.

So what was it that prevented Marco Rubio from paying off his loans before his 40s? We know it wasn't lack of income. He could have easily paid off his debt within a few years of graduation, but it took a major book deal *after* he was elected to the U.S. Senate to finally make that happen. The answer goes back to habits. Habits are a major theme to this book because they are so powerful. (Habits built in our 20s are particularly powerful.) Rubio had acquired the overconsumption lifestyle habit in college and law school. We know this because he chose to borrow heavily to pay for both. That habit, begun while in school, continued even after he began bringing in massive amounts of money. Instead of exercising control over his expenses and living below his means, Rubio's lifestyle ostensibly rose even faster than his income. By the time he made it to Washington, D.C., the Rubio family was reportedly deeply in debt for houses, cars, and consumer credit on top of his student loans.

Many students think they can avoid the pain of paying for school by delaying it until their incomes are large enough that the cost won't sting. But that is not how the world works. Instead, the habits of borrowing money and delaying pain merely grow along with their incomes. The pain can't be avoided, and the old habits can't be ignored.

So what's the big deal if students don't end up paying back their loans as quickly as they think they will? Why does that matter? As noted previously, it's a big deal because if their incomes are devoted to paying debts, that detracts from money they could be saving and investing. But the implications reach far beyond just money. Student debt influences many of the major life decisions borrowers make later, including choices about relationships, family, and career.

Million-Dollar Habits

We may not realize it, but most of our human existence is determined by our habits. We like to think we make conscious decisions about where we take our lives, but the truth is most of what we do day in and day out is controlled by what habits we have allowed to develop. The majority of our habits were begun without even realizing it.

Habits developed in the late teens and 20s can be very difficult to shake and often hang around for decades to come. Student loans are increasingly influencing the habit patterns of young adults, setting them on a life-long course to borrow and spend rather than save and invest. Those who develop and nurture the borrowing habit from the beginning of their financial life find it very difficult to reverse. This is one of the major effects of the student loan crisis which no one discusses.

The average 18-year-old kid starting college signs up for what amounts to almost forty thousand dollars' worth of debt. In other words, before most young people have learned to *save* their first dollar, they have already *borrowed* tens of thousands of dollars for school. It should come as no shock, then, that most of these individuals are not good savers when they enter the working world. The national savings rate in America is embarrassingly low, because, from the beginning, we are teaching our most educated and most productive citizens not to save money but to jumpstart the habits of borrowing and over-consuming.

Might as Well Face It, We're Addicted to Debt

We have laws on the books that prohibit young people from purchasing some products and engaging in some activities until they have reached a certain age. Have you ever considered why that is? The reason we don't allow young people to purchase alcohol, tobacco, and firearms until age 18 or 21 is because they are inadequately equipped to make those kinds of decisions. By and large their brains are not yet developed enough to appreciate the risks of interacting with those products. Alcohol is addictive and impairs judgment. Tobacco is addictive and causes cancer. Guns are dangerous and, in the wrong hands, can be devastatingly destructive. Because we know that many young people are not prepared to make wise decisions with these items, we restrict their access. Science (and decent common sense) tells us that people in their late teens and early 20s are generally less capable of dealing with dangerous and addictive substances than those who are even just a few years older. In fact, there is recent evidence that the prefrontal cortex, the part of the brain that measures risk, does not fully develop until around age 25. (Apparently the rental car companies figured this out even before the scientists.) That doesn't mean 18 or 21-year-olds aren't capable of making good decisions. It just means that, on average, they are working with inferior decision-making abilities compared to those who have been walking the earth longer.

Debt has similarities to each of the products above. Like alcohol, it can be addictive, and its potential power can distort judgment, especially for those who have never before wielded that much financial leverage. Like guns, one wrong move with debt can damage the user for a lifetime. And like tobacco, the effects may be slow, but a lifetime of usage can hamper one's ability to breathe financially and ultimately lead to financial demise if left unchecked.

What is interesting about alcohol and tobacco, specifically, are their addictive effects on the young. Studies have shown that those initially exposed to either of these substances in their teens are much more likely to become addicted than those first exposed in later adulthood. In fact, according to the CDC, nearly 9 out of 10 cigarette smokers first tried smoking by age 18, and 99% first tried smoking by age 26.[18] That's astonishing and profound. There is virtually no one addicted to smoking who started after age 26! Because of these facts, the government and nonprofits have placed much emphasis on preventing youth interaction with tobacco in hopes of preventing tobacco addiction and abuse later in life. Our first interaction with alcohol or tobacco is extremely influential on our relationship with those substances going forward. I believe that just as youth are more susceptible to developing a tobacco problem if exposed when they are young, young people are also more apt to develop an ongoing debt problem if they are trained to rely on it in their teen and early adult years.

I want to be clear, I am certainly not advocating that we use the legal system to restrict students from going into student loan debt. But we would do well to thoroughly inform young people of the risks that debt poses before sending them off to interact with this powerful and potentially addictive product. As it stands today, parents and school faculty alike usher students into the campus finance office to sign on the dotted line, generally without pause or explanation. Years later, we are surprised to find that those graduates are now mired under a mountain of debt and can't seem to get off the borrow-and-spend treadmill.

If you are a young person who is preparing to pursue a degree, please take time to consider all the risks before diving in. My goal with this book is to paint a clear picture of those risks and dangers so you can make a more educated decision.

What's the Harm in Just a Little Student Debt?

People are often shocked to hear that I think *all* higher education can and should be pursued with no debt whatsoever. Most agree that too much debt is a bad thing, but they don't see a problem with just a little bit. "What harm could a few thousand dollars bring?" they ask. Why quibble about such a small amount?

My answer is this:

A small student loan balance may not seem like a big deal. In reality, the balance itself may not be, but the trajectory that borrowing sets the student on is the bigger deal. Once again, the effects of the actions we take are often less important than the habits which those actions foster. What's the harm in borrowing 5 or 10 thousand dollars for school? What's the harm in gaining 5 or 10 pounds? Or smoking 5 or 10 cigarettes? It's not the first cigarette that kills you. It's the life-long habit of smoking that does you in. The first smoke was just the beginning of the habit. Remember, the vast majority of those who are addicted to smoking began this habit before the age of 26. Do we think it's different for debt?

Truly, habits are powerful. They are even more powerful than numbers.

Gateway Debt

A gateway drug is a drug which leads the user to more harmful and addictive drugs. It's a stepping stone to other substances. The gateway drug is the entry point which starts the user down a dangerous path.

Student loans act as *gateway debt* for many consumers. They are the first form of debt most people interact with on a large scale. Sadly, many don't even fully understand what they are getting into when they initially borrow money for school. But going deeply into student loan debt greatly increases one's chances of needing to use many other forms of borrowing later.

There are some tough practical realities that come with borrowing during the first part of life. Debt from school forces us to borrow more heavily for almost everything else going forward. If the average college student is graduating with $37,000 in debt, and the average grad student almost twice that amount, how many of these graduates are going to be willing to exercise the patience necessary to pay off their student loans before going into debt for other things? Answer: virtually none. The truth is once you've started borrowing, it's really hard to stop. Life after school throws a whole new set of expenses at the fresh graduate. The most common graduation purchase, the new car, is nearly always financed with debt. Soon after this comes marriage and kids along with a bigger car, mortgages, credit cards, and home equity loans. And so, the cycle continues. This whole string of dominoes is triggered by that initial choice to borrow for school. Life doesn't get any cheaper afterward, and it doesn't get any easier to live without debt.

So when I refer to student loans as *gateway debt*, I don't just mean that they introduce the student to the habit of borrowing. For most, student loans actually make them *dependent* on many other forms of debt for a lifetime.

Risks: Don't Say I Didn't Warn You

All debt carries risk, but student loans are extremely risky because they are speculative. The purpose of a student loan is to finance an education. The purpose of the education is to provide a career. But what happens when the education isn't completed, or the career doesn't materialize? The debt still remains. The student loan borrower is taking on an inordinate amount of risk—more than most realize.

The truth is, *our culture is prodigious at touting the benefits that come with higher education but deficient at assessing the risks that accompany education debt.* Consequently, most students only think about the potential rewards of a degree but fail to consider the risks of the debt used to acquire it. I want you to know the risks ahead of time, so you can make better decisions.

Not Everyone Graduates

Everyone who starts school intends to finish. No one would borrow money to go to college or graduate school if they weren't planning to complete the program. That would just be silly. And of course, no one would plan on failing out before they achieved their degree. Nobody plans to fail. But the reality is that not everyone who begins a program of study will finish. For various reasons, a certain percentage of students choose to drop out of school—even at the highest levels. Likewise, a certain percentage of students will fail out of college, law school, med school, etc. Not everybody gets through. According to a 2011 Harvard study, only 46% of American college students complete a four-year degree within six years.[19] That's less than half. Some research has shown that only an estimated 66% of those pursuing a two-year Master's degree complete the program within four years.[20] The four-year graduation rate for medical school has recently been found to be 81 percent.[21] These numbers aren't pretty, but they are even more sobering when you consider how many of those students took on student loans to pay for school. Not everyone who begins a program of study will ultimately graduate, but 100% of those who borrowed for school will still have to pay back their loans.

These attrition rates may not seem like a big deal. I mean, *most* students are graduating. It's better to have tried and failed than to never have tried at all, right? When student loan debt is involved, wrong. Those who took out student loans but didn't finish school are significantly worse off for their trouble. It would have been better if they hadn't gone to school at all. Then they could have at least used that time to make money and garner more career experience.

Federal Student Aid, the branch of the Federal Department of Education tasked with making higher education more affordable, has recently run a radio commercial which claims that, ". . . *after all, the most costly education is the one not begun.*" With all due respect to this organization, nothing could be further from the truth! The most costly education is NOT the one not begun. It is the one begun and financed heavily on student loans but never completed. That kind of "education" plagues the student for decades without providing any benefit.

(Un)licensed to Practice

One thing we know about the educational experience is that it never goes exactly as planned. Any number of disasters or challenges may occur.

Think this kind of stuff doesn't really happen? Think again. Sometimes it's not just getting through school that can be the major challenge, but failure to pass the necessary licensing or certification exams that can cripple a career. I graduated from law school alongside a single mom who had worked incredibly hard to get her law degree. She had a lot riding on her impending legal career. The only obstacle that stood between her and beginning her practice was the bar exam. I'm sad to report that after three attempts and more than two years removed from school, she still has not passed. That means that her big investment via student loans is still not paying off. Unfortunately, she isn't alone. The year I took the bar exam the pass rate in my state was 69.9 percent.[22] That means that after studying law for years *and* managing to graduate from law school, more than 30 percent of these highly trained and educated students were unable to get licensed, at least immediately.

It's no fun to have student loans. It's a lot less fun to have student loans and no degree or license to show for it. There is only one sure-fire method to make certain that you won't end up as one of those poor, unfortunate souls in this boat. That is to make a commitment not to take out student loans. Remove this risk from your life with one simple decision.

Some career fields require multiple degrees. These can leave the student in an extremely perilous position. What does one do with a pre-med degree? Go to medical school of course. But what happens when that option is foreclosed? Most years, more than half of the medical school applicants are not admitted to any program.[23] Yet, you must go through four years of college just to find that out. Undergraduates with a pre-law or pre-med degree who can't get into professional school still have to pay their student loans.

The Fallout: Things Don't Always Go as Planned

When students leave school it's not always for lack of effort or even ability. Often students are forced out of school for reasons completely unrelated to academics. Car wrecks and cancer don't care how much you have borrowed. They strike victims without warning and without regard to their financial situation.

During my law school orientation, I met a man who was starting law school for the third time. Twice before, cancer had knocked him out of school, but now in his mid-forties, he was still determined to finish. He was restarting because he had already made a substantial investment of both time and money in an education that was still a long way from providing a return. His circumstances were completely beyond his control.

I didn't face any major health issues, but you will remember I had some pretty close calls while in school. Even a seemingly minor hiccup like my exam scheduling mistake could easily have been a devastating disaster. My margin for error was razor thin at times. It is only by the grace of God that I didn't face more of the challenges that plague many people while in school. The academic pressure alone—particularly at the professional school level—is constant. I can only imagine the pressure that debt would add to an already extremely stressful experience.

None of us want to think about the possibility of disaster striking, but the reality is that bad things happen. When they do, they exacerbate problems with debt—particularly debt that is taken out in anticipation of degree completion. Life doesn't always wait for a more convenient time like when we are out of school. To not consider this is naïve.

The $100k Stay-at-Home Parent

The life events and changes that can force people out of school are not always negative in nature. Sometimes positive life developments can drastically shift a person's perspective on an education.

I know women who have given birth to multiple children while pursuing undergraduate and even masters or doctoral-level degrees. They have my undying respect. It *can* be done. However, I also know other families who have had the advent of children delay and even totally derail education plans. Babies are bundles of joy, but they sometimes make an unplanned appearance. Many young professionals, who planned to take the corporate world by storm, have kids and quickly find that stay-at-home parenthood is their ultimate calling. Young, single student loan borrowers soon grow into parents and their dreams change. Being a stay-at-home parent is awesome, but there is no need to incur $100k in student debt for the privilege. I only point this out because it happens more than most people realize.

America has an exceedingly well-educated stay-at-home parent population. Just think of how many men and women you know who hold college and even graduate degrees and are now staying at home with the kids. There is absolutely nothing wrong with being a stay-at-home parent. In fact, I think it is terrific for families who can afford to do so. *Afford* is the operative word though. I know many young parents who yearn to be at home with their little ones, but hefty student loan balances require both parents be active in the work force. What a tragedy that the very thing which was intended to provide opportunity and freedom often ends up being the impediment to one of life's most meaningful experiences. If these parents could go back and tell their younger selves not to borrow, do you think they would? I do.

I was listening recently to a woman who is a doctor. She wasn't practicing though. Despite $250,000 in student loans, she was staying at home with her child while her husband was working. Because her income potential was so much greater than his, she was slowly and reticently coming to the conclusion that staying at home was no longer an option for her. She had forfeited that possibility by going a quarter of a million dollars into debt. Somewhere between medical school and parenthood her dream had changed. Drastically. Now, she was being forced to give up life's most noble calling to pay for her past.

Perhaps you don't plan to ever have kids. Lots of parents once said the exact same thing. The point is life can change significantly after school. When that happens, it's much better to have options rather than obligations.

What's Gonna Happen When You Get Married?

As a happily married man, I am a zealous advocate for the institution of marriage. I would never discourage anyone from getting married who feels that they are prepared emotionally, but I do encourage those who are considering taking on large student loan balances to be aware of the challenges these debt levels can hold for a future marriage. The prospect of marriage can introduce a whole new level of risks associated with student loan debt. If marriage is something you'd like to experience in the future, before you go deeply into student loan debt as a single person, you need to be mindful that your decision now will have an impact on that relationship in the future. And the person you marry will impact your future as well. *Me* turns into *we*.

Take for instance an engaged couple I recently heard about. He is a student in medical school and she is a dental student. Together, they are going to have a combined student debt of about $600,000. $600k. Wow.

After graduation, he is set to go through four years of residency, during which time he expects to be making between $50-60 thousand per year. Her residency will be shorter, but she is three years behind him in school. In other words, it will still be several years before they can make any meaningful progress in reducing their debt balance. Meanwhile, they must figure out how to pay for a wedding, honeymoon, and all the other necessities of a newlywed life.

Of course, none of this should derail their plans for marriage. After all, the essence of marriage is facing challenges together to forge a lasting relationship. But I'd bet neither of these young professional students contemplated adding several hundred thousand dollars to their own student loan balances when they enrolled in school. Yet, it would be impossible for this level of debt not to have a substantial impact on their marriage. Together, they have bet $600,000 on their plan working perfectly. One snag could be devastating.

It's a lesson for anyone who is starting out down this path. If you are not currently married, engaged, or seriously dating, that means you don't know when or if you will meet someone or what their financial situation will be when you meet them. Marriage could easily double your debt load.

Don't take this as a warning against marriage. Take it as encouragement to avoid student loan debt for the sake of your future marriage. Being a newlywed is hard enough—having that added pressure would only add strain in combining lives.

Professional Burnout

Before I entered the legal profession or even started law school, I viewed professionals like doctors and lawyers in a completely different light than I do now. There was a certain level of mystique associated with these white-collar folks. I thought they were all rich. They're not. But I made other fallacious assumptions about them as well. I assumed they all loved their lives and got tremendous fulfillment out of their careers. I assumed they were somehow above encountering the normal dissatisfactions the rest of us face with our lower-level jobs. My time as a professional has proven my preconceptions in this area very wrong.

I first began encountering this phenomenon when I started telling other lawyers I had applied to law school. The reactions I got were often less than enthusiastic. I was shocked when *lawyers* began all but discouraging me from attending law school.

My friend Thomas was a great example of this. When I asked his advice about law school, he was a 10-year veteran attorney but had already been seeking to get out of the practice of law for some time. He had originally embarked on his legal career with great enthusiasm and idealism. Inspired by reading Harper Lee's *To Kill a Mockingbird* in high school, Thomas envisioned a legal career of fighting for the disadvantaged and upholding justice. However, a decade into his career, he was disenchanted and burnt out. Today, he runs a small business (in an unrelated field) and has given up practicing law. The fulfilling occupation he had once envisioned did not come to fruition. Thomas is not alone. Articles in legal trade publications highlight this reality across the legal landscape.

But this trend affects more than just Thomas and is broader than the legal world. A 2013 survey by NerdWallet found that most *doctors* are dissatisfied with their jobs.[24] Really? Doctors? They struggle with fulfillment too? Though it may be difficult for us to imagine, even those whose career mission is to give and preserve life and health are struggling with maintaining satisfaction in their work.

Like it or not, burnout has become a reality in many career fields, even those which we assume to be most fulfilling. This makes debt sting even more sharply.

Student loans may seem like a gift from heaven when seeking to attain a degree, but that gift becomes a scourge when you decide your chosen career isn't for you anymore. Burnout is a real risk no matter what career you ultimately pursue, but student loans magnify its effects. There's no way to know what being a lawyer, accountant, or engineer is like day in and day out until you actually do it. So you might have to go through four to eight years of school only to find out that you hate your profession.[25] The person with hefty student debt may not have a choice. They must power through. The person with no debt has options.

Debt Drives Burnout

People across all occupations are currently becoming disenchanted with their careers much faster than in the past. While I understand there are a myriad of contributing factors to this phenomenon, I think a big reason so many are becoming unfulfilled so quickly is because they feel trapped in their jobs thanks to their overbearing debt obligations. As humans, we naturally push back against anything we feel like we *have* to do. It's simply much more enjoyable and fulfilling to do things because we *want* to do them and feel we have a choice in the matter. Freedom makes everything more fun. Unfortunately, large monthly debt payments are depriving many people today from experiencing that freedom. Consequently, most people are going to work feeling more like they are fulfilling an obligation than living out a dream.

The Risks Are Real

My intention with the previous few pages was not to scare anyone out of pursuing a particular career or field of study. My only wish is to highlight the risks inherent in taking out student loans. I think overlooking these risks has contributed greatly to the runaway student loan crisis we see today. Take these warnings to heart and pay close attention to the pages that follow. As surely as there is a wrong way to pursue higher education, there is also a correct way. It *is* possible to avoid the pitfalls and garner the benefits. It just takes a little wisdom, a lot of discipline, and a lot of hard work.

The Right Risks

Just because I don't think you should borrow for school doesn't mean I don't believe in taking risks. You're in the best possible position to take risks—and reap the rewards—when you don't have debt. You should never take risks with borrowed money. That's doubly foolish. But when you have cash, you can afford to take calculated risks that have the potential for enormous gain.

Several months after I graduated from law school, Meg and I finally had our income freed up to do the things we wanted to do. For the first time, we started investing every single month. Consistent investing is the sure-fire strategy to financial prosperity. With no debt, as our income has grown, we have been able to increase our monthly investments steadily. Watching those investments grow has been one of the more gratifying experiences of our financial life. We have also been able to pour more resources into our other ventures. Cash helps moderate the risks and maximize the returns.

Costs and Consequences

We have just analyzed many of the risks associated with student loan debt. Now we are going to assess the consequences. A risk is something that *might happen.* A consequence is something that *will* happen. If you think that somehow you could borrow for school and avoid all the risks outlined above, you might be right. But you can't get around the consequences.

Everybody knows that school is expensive. Tuition and fees at most colleges and universities have been rising steadily for decades. But those who choose to finance their education with student loans will incur a slew of additional costs most borrowers never anticipate, and many of these costs are not just financial. If everyone could fully understand and internalize just how severe these costs can be, there would be far fewer student loan borrowers in the years to come.

Debt Makes Us Less Price-Sensitive

Most of us understand that people spend more when they use debt rather than cash. It has been scientifically verified that consumer spending increases with the use of things like credit cards as opposed to real money. But we tend to ignore this common sense when it comes to student loans—a much larger expense than is typically placed on a credit card. The fact of the matter is that readily available credit for student expenses has caused the average student to spend much more freely and in greater amounts than in the past when such leverage was not so easily accessible. Debt desensitizes.

Borrowed Money Is Not the Same as Earned

Borrowed money is not valued as much as earned money because the borrower doesn't have to sacrifice as the earner did. The person who pays for things with cash has already put in the time and sacrifice to earn the money and therefore understands what is required to create the value a certain amount of money represents. The borrower, on the other hand, has pushed his sacrifice into the future.

This is why it can be so easy for students to borrow such enormous amounts without giving it much thought or feeling the weight emotionally. Money is just a number to most young people. What's the difference between $50,000 and $500,000 in the mind of the average college or graduate student? Both are sums of money which these individuals have never handled before. They have no measure by which they can gauge the size and risk of borrowing large amounts.

In contrast, the person who pays with real money has a means of understanding prices much more intimately. They can mentally translate prices into the time and effort it cost them to earn a given sum of cash.

When I was making payments toward my education, I had a clear understanding of exactly what it was costing me. I understood the amount of time and work it took to earn every dollar I paid to that school. I knew that every payment converted to a certain number of lawns I had mowed or hours I had worked. It forced me to feel the value of the money I was spending. This also helped me understand that if I chose to borrow, I would simply be delaying these costs into the future. Somewhere down the line I would be forced to work a greater number of hours to pay back any amount I borrowed.

Getting Students Emotionally Invested

It can be very difficult for many 18-year-olds to emotionally comprehend how much their education really costs. Even for graduate students in their later 20s or 30s, it can be difficult to fully understand how much $100,000 is and what the repercussions are for going that deeply into debt. Most have simply never transacted business on a level that would give them any point of reference. The student who pays with cash, on the other hand, is in effect earning the right to their education as they go. This provides the tremendous value of being emotionally invested in that education.

Even for a family of means, I am a strong advocate for every student having a financial stake in their education. I just believe there is a greater sense of ownership when they have skin in the game.

Napoleon Hill, author of the mega-best-selling *Think and Grow Rich*, highlighted this phenomenon in that book. He cited the public school system in America as a "marvelous opportunity" that many students were taking for granted because it was free. Hill pointed out that, "one of the strange things about humans is that *they value only that which has a price.*"

Higher education today is certainly not free, but student loans can make it feel that way. They eliminate the sting felt when cash is forfeited. These loans have the effect of divorcing the real cost of the education from many of the students' minds. But students who are personally invested in their education and responsible for paying money out of their own pocket don't generally display this blasé attitude toward school. They understand that every minute in the classroom is costing them and that every minute in the classroom is an opportunity. Paying with cash makes the experience real and fosters a determined level of earnestness.

What College Should and Shouldn't Be

We need to recognize that college is an opportunity. It's not (or shouldn't be) an extended break from reality. During my undergraduate tenure, I was astounded at the daily lives of many of my fellow students. In fact, I'm fairly certain that several of my fraternity brothers were merely reenacting the script from *Animal House*. (If you haven't seen it, *Animal House* is a hilarious 1978 film about how *not* to do college.)

There are so many important lessons to be learned in the teens and 20s, and truthfully, most are learned *outside* the classroom. College is an opportunity to learn how to meet deadlines, sharpen people skills, gain experience, build connections, and grow in maturity. It

EVERY DEGREE DEBT FREE

shouldn't be a four-year party. Don't get me wrong, I had a blast in college and I think every student should have some fun. But we can't lose sight of what's at stake. Your 20s are the launchpad for the rest of your life.

Paying with cash helped me keep all this in perspective. It's not so tempting to toga party all night when you have work the next morning. Keg stands are really cool at 20, but what's cool at 30 is having $100,000 in the bank with no debt.

Why School Costs So Much

Increased student borrowing has repercussions not just for those who borrow, but for everyone. The government originally began subsidizing student loans as a means of making college more affordable and accessible to more people. But, as with most government involvement, there are always unintended and unforeseen consequences. One of those consequences has been the rapid increase in the cost of tuition.

The free market is an incredibly efficient mechanism. It is so efficient that when artificial stimuli are introduced, major distortions can result. For decades now, the federal government has been messing with the education market. They have made it irresponsibly easy for students to borrow unreasonable amounts of money. As a result, tuition has skyrocketed.

Why is school so expensive? Why do colleges and universities charge so much? The short answer is because students are willing to pay so much. Why are students willing to pay so much? Because they aren't really paying. Most are using borrowed money which doesn't feel real.

114

They don't feel the pain of what the education is really costing. At least, they don't feel it right away.

What else could explain why students are willing to pay more and more for degrees which are in many cases worth less and less? Many are blindly chasing a degree with no viable plan for how they will actually apply the knowledge from that degree in the marketplace. Widely available student loans have encouraged this behavior.

Government Messing with the Free Market

A chief reason tuition prices have continued to rise is because, quite frankly, student loans have induced droves of people to go after unnecessary degrees. This is basic economics. More students means greater demand, and greater demand causes prices to increase. Thanks to government aid and encouragement, the market for student loans has continued to expand. Qualification standards for loans are lax, and caps on borrowing amounts have been lifted into the stratosphere. With these kind of market manipulations, skyrocketing tuition rates shouldn't come as a surprise. We have witnessed the results of easy credit in the past. When the government relaxes mortgage lending standards and subsidizes high-risk home loans, many people begin buying houses that they shouldn't, and home prices start to rise rapidly. It is no different with higher education and student loans. Easy access to credit in the form of student debt has induced greater and greater numbers of young (and old) people to become students. In many cases it has induced the *wrong* people to go to college and graduate school.

When I say the "wrong people" I don't mean dumb

people or people who "aren't college material." There are plenty of very intelligent people currently attending college or graduate school who have no place being there.

Think about it. At the undergraduate level, there are lots of people who are not taking their education seriously. Most students enjoy college, and there is nothing wrong with that. But screwing around on student loans is bad for everyone. It wastes time and money and it drives up the cost.

Some students are taking their studies seriously, but the problem is their degree field is a joke. There simply isn't a robust market for Early French Literature majors. It's nice to collect more knowledge, but if you're not studying something which is in demand, what's the point?

Still there are others on campus today who believe that more education is what will solve all their problems. Even though the first degree hasn't paid off, they are back for another. Why? Because the numbers tell them they will make more money? No. Because student loans have made another degree that much more attainable. It's the easy answer.

Finally, for some students, school has become an escape. It has become a mechanism for delaying entry into the real world. "Why leave the comfortable confines of academia for the rough-and-tumble work life?" they ask. And with a seemingly endless student loan tab, they can continue to avoid the harsh realities of adulthood. But that's not the purpose of college and it's not even what student loans were intended for. As students are willing to spend indiscriminately more for school, colleges have begun *amenitizing*—upgrading their facilities to compete for more enrollment. Posh dorms, lavish workout facilities, and gourmet dining are the result. This can tend to make school more of a country club atmosphere than an educational experience. But it also means that the money students are paying is going more for these luxuries than actual education.

We need to understand that the easy credit handed out for student loans is one of the major reasons why tuition rates are so high today. If the leaders of our government were serious about making higher education more affordable, they would be *discouraging* rather than *encouraging* broad use of student debt. I don't think that is going to happen any time soon though. In the meantime, it's up to the consumer, the individual student, to avoid this debt on their own. Downward pressure on tuition prices will be a favor to all of us.

Effects on the Future

Student loans are affecting the lives of borrowers in ways that go beyond just finances. Young adults are pushing back major life milestones such as getting married, purchasing their first home, and even having children because payments are pinching their budgets. No one should feel they have to put off having kids or getting married because they are worried about making their student loan payments! The reality is, however, if you borrow for school, tradeoffs *will* have to be made down the line.

Heather's Dilemma

I have a good friend who is square in the middle of what I

call the "Student Loan Paradox." Her story should serve as a cautionary tale to anyone entertaining the idea of going deeply into student loan debt—even for a professional degree.

Heather is an extremely intelligent girl who made it through college without any debt, thanks to some scholarships and a little help from mom and dad. However, she decided to go on to dental school after receiving her undergraduate degree. Like most professional school students, she didn't have the funds to pay the hefty six-figure bill as she went. So, she borrowed over $200,000 to pay for her dental degree. Fortunately, she made it through the dental school program right on schedule and retained a well-paying position in a practice immediately out of school. Unfortunately, that is not the end of the story.

Shortly after beginning her practice, Heather discovered that the real world is not all it's cracked up to be. More specifically, the world of dental care is not all it's cracked up to be. She isn't enjoying being a dentist nearly as much as she thought she would. Moreover, as she is now in her late 20s, many of her friends are having babies and starting families. Heather and her husband have set the goal to pay off all her loans before they start having kids. Even at the brisk payoff pace they have set thanks to her wonderful income, the accomplishment of that goal is still many years down the road. She claims that when they finally do get the loans paid off, her goal is to either quit work or work just a couple days a week so that she can stay home with the kids. Interesting.

If the irony of this situation is lost on you, let me break it down. Here is a smart, professional young woman who has now put in eight years of higher education, including four years undergoing the rigors of *dental school*. She should be enjoying the fruits of her labor, right? But she's not. Regrettably, she has many more years of dues left to pay. What's worse is that her new plan is to give up most of the benefits of her hard-fought education virtually as soon as she's paid for it. So after eight years of high level study, she's going to spend several more years enduring a profession she's not particularly fond of, just so she can pay off the debt that financed the privilege! This is so backwards. And this is all to say nothing of the other things the pursuit of her degree has cost. If Heather and her husband indeed go through with their plan, they will essentially have given up the greater portion of their 20s and possibly 30s to pay for a degree she plans to use sparingly, if at all. And they will have delayed things like having children and buying a home. I doubt she considered this when signing her loan papers at age 22.

Heather is a prime example of what is happening to many people at both the graduate and undergraduate level today. The Student Loan Paradox is just this: We borrow heavily to go to school and get what we think will be our dream job. For a variety of reasons, many of which have to do with the student loans, our dream job doesn't turn out to be so dreamy. So we spend several years (or decades) working a job we hate until we can pay off our loans and afford to do what we love.

Wouldn't it be more efficient to just take things a little more slowly and be certain we are entering a career we enjoy without the added pressure of mounting debt?

Here is the truth about student loans: They don't enable anyone to go to school. They only enable people to go to school *faster*—which is not always better. Paying for school with cash forces the student to go slower and make more deliberate decisions about what their ultimate career will be and how they will approach their education. Student loans enable imprudence.

Adaptability in the New Economy

"Enjoying success requires the ability to adapt. Only by being open to change will you have a true opportunity to get the most from your talent."

-Nolan Ryan

Nolan Ryan is arguably the greatest pitcher in Major League Baseball history. He hurled a record 5,714 strike outs and seven career no-hitters. What is significant about Nolan Ryan though, is not only that he was such a talented pitcher, but that his career lasted so long. His time in the Major Leagues spanned four decades. Ironically, I first discovered the above quote just weeks after I had a conversation with my Uncle Mike about this Hall-of-Famer. Uncle Mike is nearly 40 years older than I am. That makes him old. He was a kid in the late 50s and early 60s and I was a kid in the 90s. I can't remember why we were discussing Nolan Ryan in the first place, but what made the conversation stick in my head was the fact that we realized Nolan Ryan was pitching in the major leagues during *both* our childhoods. That is longevity. Ryan managed to continue hurling 100-mile-an-hour fast-balls and confounding batters with his pitches through the administrations of seven different American Presidents. This dude obviously knows something about success and making success last.

Nolan Ryan made his career debut on September

11, 1966. Uncle Mike was 13. Ryan pitched his final game on September 22, 1993.[26] I was three years old, 27 years later. What allowed Ryan to last so long in the majors when the average length of a major league career is only 5.6 years? His quote explains it all. He realized that even at the top—in fact, particularly at the top—he had to maintain an ability to adapt if he was going to maintain his high level success.

Our economy is changing extremely rapidly these days. Whole industries and career fields which have thrived for hundreds of years are being replaced by new industries and career fields which we couldn't have even imagined just 20 years ago. Things aren't getting more predictable and more certain; things are getting less predictable and less certain. That's not necessarily a bad thing. Most of the changes which have taken place in our economy in recent decades have been for the good. We have developed more products and innovations which make work less cumbersome and life more convenient. But some people have been caught amidst the changes and suffered for it. They are the ones who weren't prepared and couldn't adapt quickly.

Obligations Are the Enemy of Opportunity

As the pace of change accelerates, obligations become even more weighty. Anything that holds us back from being nimble and adaptable prevents us from taking advantage of opportunities when they arise. This will be the unforeseen price paid by those mired in student loan debt. Opportunities will come, and many people will lose out because their resources are already devoted elsewhere.

On the flip side, avoiding debt is the best way to be ready to take advantage of opportunities in a fast moving economy. If we want to maximize our success, we need to maintain the ability to tweak our careers to evolve with the times. The old days of working the same job for 40 years and retiring with a gold watch are over. The average worker today will have 10 different jobs before the age of 40.[27] According to the Washington Post, only 27% of college graduates have a job related to their major.[28] That doesn't mean we won't always be using some of the knowledge we learned in college or graduate school, but it does mean we will be called on to acquire new knowledge or education in different areas. Rather than being married to a certain career, we need to admit that our careers and education will likely be ever-evolving. Debt only stifles our ability to take advantage of these new opportunities.

Painful Irony

Young professionals today crave an environment that offers freedom to work on a more liberated schedule. Additionally, we balk at the notion that work is simply about bringing home a paycheck. Our awareness of social causes and desire for influence has instilled a need to feel that what we do every day matters. We yearn for meaning in our work and believe that our daily toil should have purpose. For our parents, work was about stability and a paycheck. For us, work is about flexibility and fulfillment.

Student loans stand as a stark adversary to these ideals. They stifle flexibility in the marketplace and distract from purpose and meaning. *It's not very fulfilling to perform a job merely to pay back student loans.*

The Death of Idealism

I am convinced that one of the most tragic casualties of the student loan crisis is the loss of creative capital in the minds of young people. It's difficult to find the energy and motivation to achieve new things when your resources are devoted to paying back debt. Student loans are robbing an ambitious and optimistic generation of its fight. Twenty-something idealists are being turned into cynics by the time they reach 30. What ideas, innovations, and contributions are we missing out on because of this? I fear we may never know.

What does this loss of creative energy look like? It's a person working a job they don't want to work just to pay their student loan bill. It's an entrepreneur not being able to take risks because his resources are already obligated. It's a young couple not able to move to a new city or start a new business because they are so deeply in debt. It's the aspiring author who can't find time to write the next best-seller because she is working two or three jobs. I could go on and on, but I don't need to. You know people who are in this exact situation. They have dreams and they would follow them, but then how would they pay their loans? This is one of the costs no one ever discusses.

Most people who pursue an undergraduate or graduate education do so for the right reasons. They want to make money and have a good standard of living, yes, but above all, they want to help people. That's why a medical student spends countless hours studying or an aspiring educator invests so much time student teaching.

The truth is we need good doctors and lawyers and dentists and business people. We need good nurses and teachers and engineers. And we need them to be free. We need them to be nimble enough to follow their passions and God's calling. We need YOU to be free. We *don't* need you shackled by student loans.

We Really Can Have It All

As modern young professionals, we are audacious enough to believe we can have careers we love that give our lives meaning *and* make a difference in our world. And in truth we are the first generation that has reason to believe all this can be achieved on a widespread basis. The only thing that could stop us is if we chose to give that freedom and opportunity away ourselves.

Americans born after the year 1980 have the distinct privilege of being the first generation in the history of the world which has grown up with the *expectation* of achieving a college-level education. That's quite astounding. There have literally been hundreds of generations of humans for which this was not the reality. For our parents, college was becoming more attainable, but the majority of people still didn't pursue it. In our grandparents' generation, almost no one went to college. This is very important to consider. One of the main reasons our grandparents didn't go to college was because they couldn't afford it. It was simply out of the question financially.

Today, as student loans become more and more prevalent, it seems everyone has begun to believe that they both *can* and *should* go to college and perhaps even graduate school.

Education Overvalued?

We have come to believe this so fervently that many people have convinced themselves that higher education should be acquired at all costs. The increased availability of something which was for so long out of reach has created a gold rush of sorts, with many abandoning sound reasoning to pursue formal education, even if it means borrowing to the hilt. However, just like in 1849, all that glitters is not gold.

While information and knowledge are more valuable than ever, in many ways, *formal* education has become substantially *overvalued*. Certainly a college or graduate degree can be the key that opens the door of opportunity; but blindly pursuing education for education's sake is of no benefit to anyone.

We have come to view higher education as a box we check that is supposed to guarantee success. But a college degree is not a meal ticket. It's an admission ticket which will get you in the door. The rest is up to you.

From Nonprofit Idealist to Cynical Mercenary

I was recently made aware of a very sad story. A girl had graduated from college and was working at a non-profit agency. But because she had borrowed so heavily to get through school, she was not able to make even the minimum payments on her student loans. She was passionate about the work she was doing and felt called to be doing it, but reality was slapping her in face. She had dreamed of doing this kind of work for a long time and had even put in the long hours of study required to achieve a degree in that field. But the truth was she had forfeited her dream (at least temporarily) when she took out enormous student loans to achieve it. Her primary concern had to be making money. Her massive student debt was forcing her to transition from an idealist to a mercenary.

I'm afraid this story is becoming all too commonplace in America.

We are a generation of idealists. Many of us intend to use our educations to further social justice causes, catalyze change, *and* make a great economic life for ourselves. We believe we can have it all. And I believe we can as well, but not necessarily as quickly as we might think we deserve. As a generation, we have fallen prey to believing we can change the world while not accepting that we may have to first pay the price of patience and hard work to achieve our noble ambitions. There is an element of entitlement in this attitude. We think we automatically deserve a job that provides a healthy wage *and* meaning *and* fulfillment. But the opportunity to do such fulfilling work is not a right. It's a privilege. Most of us will have to *earn* that privilege and the ability to live out our dreams—even if those dreams are noble and altruistic.

Debt Keeps You from Your Calling

I'm a Christ-follower and having the ability to answer God's call is a big deal to me. You never know when or where He may call you. He is kind of known for that. This is a major reason I was committed to getting my education without debt. I didn't want to be obligated to anything but His will. I figured that if He wanted me to get a law degree, He would provide a way to do it without borrowing. He did. And He gave me the opportunity to learn a whole lot of other things in the process. Now, I am free to respond to His direction without hindrance or hesitation.

I firmly believe we are all called to something in this life. I want to help you to be free to answer that call. For too many people today, the shackles of student loans are holding them back. That doesn't have to be you.

The problem with not pursuing your calling is not only what it means for you. The bigger problem is that it deprives the world of the gifts which only you can provide. When you don't, *or can't*, pursue your calling, you aren't just doing a disservice to yourself. You are doing a disservice to all of us.

Finding what you were meant to do can be an arduous journey and often is a process of elimination. Most people don't know what they want their ultimate career to be even after they've graduated college. We know this because the average person changes jobs every 4.4 years and, as mentioned earlier, only 27.3% of college graduates have a job related to their major.[2930] For many, the time in school and immediately after is a period of experimentation, exploration, and discovery. But getting saddled with student loan debt is a good way to stifle this process. Working and paying cash may be the most efficient method of fleshing out our passions.

Mother, Should I Trust the Government?

A lot of people today are looking to the government to mend the student loan crisis. They believe some quick political fixes are all it will take to rectify this debacle. Those who have already racked up a pile of student loans are looking to the government for relief through various forgiveness programs, and some are even hoping that Congress will step in and cancel their debts altogether.

Others, who are only now considering taking out student loans, look to government forgiveness plans as a justification for borrowing. They are counting on certain programs and hoped-for political action to be there if they can't pay off their loans on their own.

Due to the growing number of people affected by this epidemic and the fact that many of them are getting older (statistically more politically active and powerful), more and more politicians are giving lip service to what can be done to address the matter. It has become a political football and will continue to be even more so in the future. Sadly, however, I have bad news for those of you who are waiting on the government to forgive your loans or are entertaining the idea of going into student debt thinking that the government will someday forgive your loans—it's not going to happen.

Counting on the government to remedy the student loan crisis is a fool's errand. They simply aren't capable.

Remember, *the government created the problem in the first place*! Why do we now look to them to fix it? The student loan crisis will only be fixed when we, as a nation, come to understand that it is up to *us* to fix. The problem may have been initiated and perpetuated by short-sighted bureaucrats, but it will only be remedied by wise and decisive action on the part of individuals. It's not up to them, it's up to us.

Loan Forgiveness Programs Are a Joke

Student loan forgiveness plans have become more and more prominent in recent years. While these options may seem like a method of avoiding the pains associated with student debt, there are a lot of reasons these plans are far less attractive than they first appear.

Most programs require the borrower to remain employed in a certain field or in a specific geographic location with a nonprofit or government agency. Usually, these are jobs for which there is a shortage, because it is hard to get people to do them. The borrower must make a prescribed number of payments over many years, after which the remaining balance of their federal student loans is forgiven. There are always catches, however.

I won't go into the details of each program, but suffice it to say, they tend to keep the borrower in debt for a very long time (10 to 30 years), carry enormous risk (one missed payment can derail the entire plan), and require the graduate to work in an area or at a salary significantly less than in the open market.

To sum it up, student loan forgiveness offerings are a poor attempt by the federal government to rectify decades of disastrous policy. The government has already hinted that it may not honor some of these programs, even after the student has completed all the requirements. What? The government not doing what it promised? Shocking! But then again, the government doesn't have to honor its promises. It's the government, after all. The moral of the story is this—don't arrange your life hoping the government will swoop in and save the day. Pay with cash and make these programs irrelevant.

Student Loan Debt Is NOT Inevitable

I hear a lot of people say things like, "I *had* to go into debt . . ." But no one ever *has* to borrow money—especially for school. What they should admit is that they *chose* to borrow. Debt is always a choice, it's never an inevitability. The price of avoiding debt is hard work and patience. The cost of going into debt is your future. We are never forced into debt. I think way too many people today—both students and parents of students—see school debt as unavoidable, but that couldn't be further from the truth.

In the next section, you will get to know stories of people who did not accept the notion that higher education requires student loans. These people desired a great education, but unlike most of their peers, would not accept debt as the means to achieve it. The best part is that each of these graduates is now living the life they dreamed of. Several have already achieved massive success due in major part to the fact that their educations have been assets rather than hindrances. These same opportunities are available to you.

It's Easier to Do Today Than Ever Before

Many people claim that it's harder to go to school without debt than ever before. My contention is that it is more *achievable* now than ever. Higher education is far more widespread and available than in the past. If you really want a college or graduate degree, it's more accessible, more available, more flexible, and consequently, more affordable today than it ever has been.

If you don't believe me, just keep reading.

PART THREE

HOW ANYONE CAN DO IT: PROVEN STRATEGIES FOR GRADUATING DEBT FREE

The people who get on in this world are the people who get up and look for the circumstances they want and if they can't find them, make them.

-George Bernard Shaw

Early in this book I stated that one of the underlying causes of the student loan crisis was a lack of planning. Students and parents are doing a poor job of preparing in advance to pay for higher education. As a result, the average student is taking out mountains of debt. Obviously, the earlier one begins to plan, the better. Time is a tremendous ally. However, even for those with little to no time until school begins, a carefully crafted plan can be the difference between decades of debt and a future of freedom. The key is to deliberately assess all factors relating to how much school will cost, identify which costs can be avoided, and what income sources are available to pay those costs. In this section we will take a thorough look at these factors, and I will attempt to relay the helpful tips and advice that have allowed me and many others to graduate without debt.

Make the Commitment

The most crucial step for going to school without debt is to *commit* to not borrowing. This decision must be made in advance. Otherwise, when the going gets tough, and it will, you will cave. Remove this option from the table. Then, other options will appear.

#1- Select a School You Can Afford

Choice of school is the largest variable in the college or graduate school cost equation and it has implications far beyond just tuition. The good news is that this allows the greatest opportunity to swing the numbers to your advantage. There is a vast array of tuition rates and additional costs that vary dramatically depending on the institution. This makes school choice absolutely critical. Also, remember that "afford" doesn't mean that you *think* you can pay for it or that you can pay for a semester or two. It means that you have a realistic plan for paying cash for the entire program.

If it doesn't at first appear that there are any schools you can afford, that doesn't mean you can't go to school or that you are pigeon-holed into borrowing. It simply means you haven't dug up enough options. There are always more options out there. It may mean you need more time. Often students feel immense pressure to immediately enroll in one of the schools to which they are initially accepted. We will talk more about the value of being willing to wait later, but for now, suffice it to say that taking the time to get accepted to a more affordable school may be one of the most profitable decisions any student can make.

Public vs. Private

Many students get hung up on the desire to attend a prestigious private college or university. Some people who walk around with their noses protruding into the air even believe that a quality education *can't* be attained at a public university. Nothing could be further from the truth. Certainly, many private colleges offer quality educations. They usually carry high-dollar price tags as well. While significantly more affordable, many state universities offer a strong academic environment which is more than sufficient to provide a quality education.

For my undergraduate education, I attended one of

the top-ranked private colleges in my state. For my law school experience, I opted for one of the larger public universities. In neither case did my selection rely heavily upon the school's reputation. The number one factor in my decision was price. By *price,* I don't mean the sticker price of the school. There is a vast difference between sticker price and real cost. It is essential to remember that thanks to scholarships and financial aid, the cost of a specific school will vary for each student. The average total cost at a private, four-year college was $38,589 in 2011, compared with $17,000 at the average public institution.[31] In general, public schools will be less expensive than private institutions, and lower-tier colleges cheaper than so-called prestigious universities, but these must be evaluated on an individual basis.

My decision to attend a private college resulted from the fact that it was actually more affordable for *me* than my local state university. Despite the fact that the state school (the University of Kentucky) offered drastically lower sticker-price tuition, the additional scholarships and aid I received from the private liberal arts school (Georgetown College) resulted in a lower price tag for me. Therefore, I generally encourage students to apply to at least three schools, two of which should be state universities.

There is no evidence which indicates that graduates of private schools are more successful than those who graduate from public institutions. Think about it. You know plenty of successful doctors, lawyers, engineers and other professionals who graduated from state schools. Odds are, you know more successful public school graduates than private school graduates. There is nothing wrong with a private education. But a degree from a public school usually provides the same benefits at a substantially reduced cost.

In-State vs. Out-of-State

There is no question that when all things are equal it is more affordable to attend a college or university within your state rather than outside it. Out-of-state tuition is, on average, more than double the cost of tuition at comparable in-state schools.[32]

I struggle to comprehend any justification for paying out-of-state tuition for college or graduate school unless you possess a boatload of cash and a great reason to burn it. Outside of extenuating circumstances (i.e. a great scholarship, a specialized program of study is not available in your state, etc.) in-state schools offer a drastically less expensive option versus comparable out-of-state institutions.

Prestige vs. Non-Prestige

Many students (and their parents) make the mistake of selecting a school based largely upon its reputation or academic prestige. This line of thinking probably results in more student debt than just about any other. The truth of the matter is that once you have a degree, very few people care *where* you went to school. Harvard and Yale produce a lot of successful graduates. But so does your local state school. Understand that paying for prestige is just that. When you pay for an undergraduate or graduate degree, you should be paying for knowledge. The quality of the education is more a result of the dedication of the student than the ranking of the school.

Keep in mind that when surveyed, six out of seven millionaires did not indicate that "attending a top-rated college" was very important in explaining their economic success.[33] This is probably because 80% of millionaires never attended a so-called top rated undergraduate program.[34] Again, there is simply no data to indicate that school prestige is a determinative factor for a graduate's future success. Therefore, if you decide to pay more for prestige, that's fine. But understand that decision is based more on enhancing your ego than your pocketbook.

Alternatives to the Traditional Four-Year Degree

Community College

Community college represents a fantastic opportunity for many students to quickly attain a degree in a marketable field or to knock out their first two years of undergraduate at an exceptionally affordable rate. Some states are now even offering free community college to all residents. The prospect of graduating in two years with the ability to immediately enter the marketplace and make money should not be overlooked. The right degree from a community college can have a tremendous return on time and money spent. Don't be a snob. Consider this option.

Community college can also be an inexpensive source of additional credits to put toward a traditional college degree. Many of these classes transfer to the major universities. There is no reason to pay $900 per credit hour at the university when you can acquire the same credit for $50 per hour at the community college.

Technical Schools

Closely related to community colleges are vocational or technical schools. These institutions train students for immediate employment in a specific trade. America is in dire need of skilled workers like welders, electricians, masons, HVAC professionals, and a host of other tradespersons. If you are a young person coming out of high school, I strongly suggest you consider this route. You will be out of school and making money while your college friends are still sitting in the classroom and paying tuition. As a bonus, the cost of these types of programs is generally extremely reasonable. You will have in-demand skills and a head start on your earning career.

Saving Big by Cutting College Short

Our educational system has boxed everyone into a one-size-fits-all model. But no student's situation is exactly like any other student's situation. Most people don't realize how much money can be saved simply by bucking the traditional academic calendar.

There are a lot of ways to hack the system. One of the most effective is to maximize credits and cut the experience as short as possible. The more time spent on campus, the more money is spent. When it comes to higher education, credits are quite literally money. They are the currency of academia. The goal is to collect credit hours as efficiently as possible. It doesn't require four years to graduate college; it requires 120 credit hours. Every 15 hours of credit the student can acquire is another semester's worth of tuition that can be avoided. Fortunately, there are a slew of sources available for gaining credits, many of which are very cheap or even free.

Students can start earning college credit as early as high school with dual credit or Advanced Placement courses. These same courses could cost hundreds of dollars per hour if taken as an enrolled college student but are often free or substantially discounted in high school. Likewise, many high school students have the opportunity to attend classes at local community colleges. So long as these classes transfer to your university of choice, this can be another source of inexpensive college credit. During my senior year of high school, I took three classes at the community college in my hometown. These classes all transferred to my four-year school and counted as 9 of my required 120 hours.

Even after the student has enrolled in college, sources of inexpensive credits are still available. CLEP tests are exams that allow the student to prove his or her knowledge by passing a standardized exam to take the place of many introductory college courses. A passing score can earn the student three or more credit hours per test. This is huge because the fee for each CLEP exam is less than $100, but the same course will likely cost hundreds if taken at a four-year institution. I took multiple CLEP exams while in college and it saved me some serious time and money. My only regret is that I didn't take more!

It only takes 15 hours per semester to graduate in four years, but it is my belief that the average college student can easily handle more than 15 hours of classroom time each week. Bumping up to merely 18 hours would allow the student to graduate a full semester early, saving thousands. After my first semester of college, I took at least 18 hours every single term—sometimes as many as

21. This, coupled with my high school credits and CLEP exams, allowed me to graduate in seven semesters rather than eight and also gain a double major.

#2- Analyze the ROI of Your Education

Although we don't always think in these terms, a formal education is an investment and should be treated as one. In other words, it's a business decision. All investments are made to reap a return. When you invest money, the goal is to ultimately get your money back at an increase. This is called a return on investment, or ROI. An education can have multiple returns, but the primary ROI should be money in the form of increased earning power.

Some people will argue that acquiring more education results in gratification and personal growth. This is undeniably true. However, gratification and personal growth can also be attained by a trip to the local library. We would not ordinarily pay for that kind of education. Education stemming from a college degree needs to have an appreciable financial return. Otherwise, we are wasting money on tuition.

One method which is helpful for efficiently assessing the ROI of an education is simple cost-benefit analysis. What are you getting for what you are spending? Formal education costs a lot—not just in terms of money. Much time and energy are also involved in getting a degree. We need to make certain that the costs we are paying are worth the benefits we are receiving.

Break-Even Analysis

One way to measure the profitability of any investment is to assess how quickly your initial investment will be returned—the point at which you will break even. This is conveniently termed *Break-Even Analysis*.

For higher education your break-even point is that moment at which the added income you can make after attaining a degree equals the amount of money that you spent getting that degree. If a degree is going to allow you to make $20,000 more per year and school costs $100,000, your break-even point would be five years (5 x $20,000 = $100,000). Notice that this analysis does not consider how much you could make in total, it only considers how much *more* you can make after getting that degree. In other words, how much financial benefit does the degree add over and above your existing income potential? If you can make $30,000 per year now, but $50,000 with a bachelor's degree, the ROI of that degree is not $50,000 per year, its only $20,000. That's important to remember.

The analysis we did above is oversimplified though, because it doesn't consider *all* the costs. For example, it ignored what economists call *opportunity cost*. This is the income a student *gives up* when he decides to attend school. If the student could make $30,000 per year working full time, but can only make $15,000 per year while in school, then the opportunity cost of a four-year degree would be an additional $60,000 (4 x $15,000). Added to the break-even analysis above, this would extend his break-even point from five years to eight years. That means he will have to use his degree for *eight years before he sees the first dollar in return.* That is sobering to think about.

This type of analysis can be extremely pertinent to those considering a graduate or professional degree. If you are a college graduate who is currently marketable at $50,000 per year, but you intend to get a law degree which will enable you to make $100,000 per year, then the benefit of that move will be $50,000 annually. However, if law school costs $200,000, and you are planning to go to school full time without working for three years, then the opportunity cost of that lost income will be an additional $150,000. So the total cost of your law degree will be $350,000 ($200,000 for law school + $150,000 of lost income during school). With an income benefit of $50,000 per year, it will take seven years after graduation to see your first dollar of net positive return. If that money was borrowed, interest and fees will push the break-even point out much further.

Break-even analysis isn't the determining factor when considering additional education, but it shouldn't be ignored either. It can be extremely helpful in assessing whether the return on education is worth the investment.

#3- Choose a Marketable Degree Field

It's vital that all students make certain that the knowledge and skills they get from a degree are in-demand in the marketplace. It's shocking how little thought many give to this aspect of their education. Contrary to a lot of the popular, feel-good messages out there, you should not select a field of study just because you love it.

There are basically only three reasons to pursue formal education: to make more money, to make a difference, and to make life more meaningful. It's difficult to make a difference in the world if you can't pay your bills. Choose a degree because you believe you will be fulfilled working in that area for decades to come, *and* it has a proven, sustainable financial return. Meaning and fulfillment will suffer if the income isn't there.

Fortunately, plentiful data is available on industry averages for most degree fields. These statistics can provide a good idea of how much the average graduate in a specific industry can expect to make. Be sure to pay attention to how this varies depending on geographic location. Salaries in New York or California will usually exceed salaries for the same career in the Midwest. Likewise, understand that it will probably take time for the fresh graduate to work up to the industry average. As I highlighted in a previous section, even lawyers are generally required to put in several years as a junior associate before their incomes really begin to take off, and most doctors spend several years in residency before they break into the six-figure range. The same is true for most career fields. Make certain that you are familiar with not only the industry averages but also the specific levels of experience which are required to reach those incomes.

Before you begin pursuing a degree, you need to be reasonably certain that it will provide an opportunity for a job upon graduation and a long-term career path thereafter. General areas of study like business or communications provide a wide array of viable options. Some specialized degree fields can be extremely lucrative, but others are abysmally unprofitable. Be smart and spend ample time selecting your field of study carefully.

#4- Fully Assess ALL Costs
(And Determine Which Can Be Avoided)

The benefits of an education are obvious. Most of us don't have trouble understanding the value a degree can produce for the graduate. However, as a general rule, most prospective students are not adept at thoroughly assessing *all* the costs of an education. Understanding the complete cost picture is just as important as understanding the benefits. But recognizing *which costs can be avoided* is most crucial of all.

As you have likely surmised, one of the central themes of this book is that you should not let others set your expectations for you. When it comes to higher education, it is wise to question most everything anyone says—particularly those who work for the schools. This advice will be exceptionally handy when assessing what colleges and universities refer to as "cost of attendance."

Cost of attendance is a broad term which is generally intended to include not only tuition and books, but virtually anything that is even loosely associated with the school experience. Each year most universities publish an estimate of what they believe it will cost to attend their particular institution. By and large I find these projections to be astronomically high. Any student who is willing to keep even a loose rein on expenses can generally live on substantially less than the school website suggests—often less than half.

Publishing an estimated cost of attendance is intended as a helpful gesture, but these estimates are prepared *by* average consumers *for* average consumers. *You* are not the average consumer. Relying exclusively on these numbers is a pathway to student loan land. Most prospective students read these estimates and immediately assume a debt-free education simply isn't possible for them. Others take these numbers for granted and mindlessly spend vastly more than is necessary. Remember, allowing others to set your expectations for you is often devastating to your success.

Allow me to illustrate the potential pitfalls of relying on your university to set the expectations for what you will spend and how much you will "need" to borrow. For the purposes of this discussion, I will use numbers from my school at the time I was enrolled there. During the 2013-2014 academic year, according to my law school's website, the estimated cost of attendance was $53,614.[35] This translated to a total debt-financed cost over three years of $204,989, according to The Law School Transparency.[36] These numbers are comparable to most other public law schools and are what the prospective student sees when making decisions about whether and how much to borrow. But let's break down what these numbers really mean.

The biggest single component in cost of attendance is tuition. For the year of 2013-2014, tuition at the University of Louisville School of Law was just under $20,000. That leaves more than $30,000 estimated to cover living expenses. "Living expenses" is another catchall term schools use that can mean virtually anything, including extracurricular activities. One would think this term refers mostly to food, shelter, and transportation—the necessities of life, correct? But let's take a closer look at what the schools are lumping into the "living expenses" category.

Along with "room and board" and "books and supplies," my school's website also suggested making allowance for the categories of "personal expenses," amounting to almost $5,000, "travel"—over $3,000, and "Stafford loan fees" in the amount of $198. My first question is: What in the world are "personal expenses" and why would I need almost five thousand dollars to cover them? When I was in school I ate, slept, studied, and worked. I simply didn't have time for personal expenses. I did know some girls who liked to get their nails done and some dudes who enjoyed a regular round of golf—maybe those are the personal expenses the school was anticipating. "Travel" is another expense I wasn't familiar with. I could have seen a lot on three thousand dollars, but I'm not sure what student needs to be travelling anywhere other than school, work, and home. If your parents want to see you for the holidays, they can cover the cost of a plane ticket. Other than that, you can travel *after* you graduate. Finally, there is the suggested Stafford Loan Fee of $198. I love that the school is helping to warm new students up to the idea that they will be charged a fee for the privilege of later getting charged interest. No thanks, I'll skip that one as well.

Now don't get me wrong, I'm well aware that every student will encounter annual expenses beyond room, board, and tuition. Planning for unexpected costs is wise. But taking for granted that a school's suggested cost of attendance is how much it will cost *you* to attend is downright foolish. The point is much of what is driving the student loans crisis in America and what will drive you into student loan debt if you let it, is allowing other people to determine what is normal and what is required for you.

Again, I think schools generally publish numbers

like these with helpful intentions, but the practical result can be very damaging. Projecting "average" figures at this level for prospective students is a way of normalizing massive student loan debt.

What would have happened if I had taken my school's numbers and assumptions for granted? Based on the school's projected cost of attendance, I should have expected to pay (finance) over $200,000 for my law degree. My $15,000 per year scholarship meant I could avoid $45,000 of this debt, but that still would have left me with over $150,000 to pay back. That figure is dangerously close to the average debt for law school graduates. But these were presuppositions I was simply unwilling to accept. I knew I could live on much less than the average student and on *drastically* less than the law school's website suggested.

The natural instinct of admissions officers and the school finance department is going to be to push you into student loans. Most just can't conceive of another way. But keep in mind, these people won't be making your student loan payments—you will be.

In my case, the discrepancy between the school's estimates and what it actually cost *me* was gargantuan. While tuition was unavoidable, I was able to get by on a fraction of what they had estimated for everything else.

Half of the "cost of attendance" really isn't cost of attendance at all. It's the cost of life. We all have living expenses whether we are in school or not. Most students are living at a pretty high standard in college and graduate school. There's lots of room for savings. The key is to think for yourself and practice frugality while in school. I promise, it'll be worth it.

#5- Live Like a Student While You're in School

Stop acting like a lawyer (You're not one yet!)

The most important thing I learned in law school didn't come out of a textbook or class lecture. It was uttered by the head dean at an assembly of our entire class. She cautioned us 1st-year students about the pitfalls of letting our lifestyles get out of control before graduation. She said, "If you live like a lawyer in law school, you'll be living like a law student as a lawyer. But if you live like a law student in law school, you'll have your whole life to live like a lawyer after you graduate." This phrase can be adapted to fit just about any profession: doctor, dentist, engineer, teacher, etc. Student loans can allow students to live a lifestyle far above that which they should be living while in school. This can have a lingering impact on their financial future. However, a few short years of frugality will allow the young professional to leverage their career thereafter, resulting in lifelong prosperity. School is not the time you are to be living the life. It is the time you are to be getting the job done. If you are still in school, you haven't made it yet. Don't act like you have.

Dave Ramsey likes to say that we as humans have four basic needs: food, clothing, transportation, and shelter. Everything beyond that is a luxury. The funny thing is, while those four things are required to survive, there is a vast range of prices you can pay for any one of those items. While in school, your objective should be to hold each of these to the absolute minimum. You are in survival mode until graduation. Minimalism is the name of the game. When I was in law school, I was shocked at what many of my fellow students (particularly those who were financing life with student loans) would spend money on.

I distinctly recall one Monday morning when two of my cohorts were casually discussing the bar they had patronized the previous Saturday night and the twenty-dollar drinks they had consumed there. I would have been surprised, but then again one of these individuals was the same girl I had observed shopping on her laptop in the middle of our Property Law class a week earlier. Her online retailer of choice: Vineyard Vines.

I want to be clear, I'm not against nice clothes or fine food and drink . . . when purchased by people who have earned the right. Most students are not those people. There's plenty of time to indulge in those purchases post-graduation. A tab of twenty-dollar drinks financed on a Sallie Mae loan is the epitome of highly-educated stupidity.

Living Expenses

Living expenses are the component of school cost which can most easily be controlled. As we have noted, you need a place to live whether you're in school or not. We know it can be done much cheaper than most schools suggest. If you are a college student who can still live at home with your parents or you are married and living with a spouse, massive amounts of money can be saved. It just doesn't take that much money to survive in most parts of the country.

In college, if you must live on campus or near the school, dorms are often the most affordable option. Most major universities are surrounded by luxurious apartment complexes intended to lure the students with more discriminating tastes away from bland old dorm life. Some even include amenities like tennis courts, pools, coffee shops, and spas. While the temptation can be great, I implore you to "keep living like a student" and avoid this pitfall. Personally, I think half the excitement of college was living in a 12'x15' room that bore a striking resemblance to a jail cell. What could be more fun? At the very least, if you are sick of dorm living, see if you can lessen the expense by sharing a rental with multiple roommates. The equation for cheaper rent is very simple: more roommates = less rent. So get a rental house you can share with 12 roommates. Rent will be negligible. Boom.

Those in a post-graduate setting don't usually have the dorm room option available and are generally less amenable to the *Animal House* antics the multiple-roommate situation may present. Grad students will undoubtedly seek a more mature atmosphere than their undergraduate counterparts, but there is no reason this can't also be inexpensive. Until I got married, I rented that room from Steve for $300 per month during my first year of law school. After that Meg and I lived in the cheapest decent apartment we could find. Both locales offered clean, comfortable quarters and plenty of quiet space for studying. I didn't need to drop two grand a month on a place just because I was in law school. You don't either.

Transportation (Ode to the 4Runner)

In most parts of the country, a car is somewhat of a necessity. But I see a lot of college and graduate students driving around in much more than is necessary. While many students spend way too much money on this category, reliable transportation doesn't have to be expensive and it can even be profitable.

During most of my undergraduate tenure, I drove a $300, 20-year-old Honda Accord. It was mechanically sound, but long ago both the AC and heat had quit working, and the muffler had fallen off. My friends could hear me approaching from a mile away. It's most striking feature, however, was the fact that the driver's side door was permanently locked and wouldn't open. So to get in, I had to slide over from the passenger seat or enter through the driver's window Nascar-style. It was a real gem. Fortunately, during my senior year of college, I upgraded considerably. Because I paid cash, I was able to buy a 1998 Toyota 4Runner for $3700, which was about half the amount of its book value. To most people, this vehicle probably appeared to be just another old used car. But to me, it was everything.

To date, I consider that car one of my wisest purchases. I spent only the cash I had on hand and utilized patience and discipline to get a great deal. The car was a workhorse for me, pulling double duty as a highway-driver to and from my law school classes and a trailer-puller when towing my mowing equipment. It wasn't just a car; it was a money-maker. With it I delivered pizzas, towed a mower, ripped out bushes, transported tools, showed houses, and hauled all sorts of things for money. Five years later, the car had carried me through college and law school and had given me over 100,000 miles of relentless utility. It didn't sparkle but it got the job done.

The point here is that during school a car isn't a luxury, it's a tool. It's a business expense, and every dime you spend more than necessary is one that could have been devoted to a more noble goal. Drive something that is commensurate with your needs and lends itself to side-hustling. Besides, college is the time when you're *supposed* to cruise around in a piece of junk. Nobody expects anything different. So own a cheap, useful car while you're in school. Soak it up. Drive like a student while you're in school so you can drive like a professional when you're out.

Books

The cost of textbooks for college-level courses is astronomically high. If you have attended one day's worth of classes, you understand this. However, books are an expense on which many students don't realize they can save a considerable amount of money. While cases will vary, many classes in college never actually use the textbooks listed as "required" in the syllabus. Some professors only test from lectures while others never even assign reading. It's a waste of money to buy a book that is never used. My strategy was to wait until the first class, assess whether or not the textbook would actually be used, and purchase only if necessary. Even if I deduced that the textbook was indeed necessary, I would always attempt to purchase a used version from Amazon or maybe even share the cost of the book with another student.

You may be surprised to know that this strategy was applicable in law school as well. For certain, there were fewer classes in which I could get by without a book, but some still just weren't necessary. I once again saved hundreds of dollars buying used rather than new. College textbooks are a racket. You can't always avoid this expense, but if you are careful, you can beat the system more times than not.

Don't be like my classmate who bragged about

purchasing all her law books a month before the semester began for the tidy sum of $1,700. By waiting, I managed to buy the exact same books for under $300.

The Payback: Interest

One of the best reasons to pay cash for school is that paying cash is a sure-fire strategy for avoiding paying interest. Interest on student loans is killer. As we've seen, the average college graduate in 2016 left school with a loan balance of $37,172, and it takes the average student loan borrower about 21 years to fully repay their loans. At seven percent interest per year (many borrowers pay more), this would mean the average student borrower ends up paying back over $71,000 for an original bill that was only about half that amount.

It gets worse for graduate-level borrowers. My friend Kyle is a great example. Kyle graduated from law school 15 years ago. When he graduated, the school was kind enough to grant him not only a diploma but also $105,000 worth of student debt—pretty typical for law school graduates at the time. His loan balance was placed on a 30-year repayment schedule with monthly payments of approximately $700. For 15 years, Kyle has made his payment every single month. That's 180 months! In other words, he has now paid over $126,000 back toward his loan balance. However, his principal has only been reduced to $90,000! He still has a long way to go. In summary, the degree that would only have cost about $100,000, if paid for in cash, will end up costing Kyle more than $250,000 when it's all said and done.

Paying cash saves incredible amounts of money.

Paying: It's Usually a Combination of Things

I don't know exactly what your path to a debt-free degree will look like, but it probably won't look exactly like mine or anyone else's, and there probably won't be one thing that pushes you over the top. *Most people who successfully pay for college or a graduate degree without loans do so using a combination of methods.* They cobble together resources from several different areas. Most students won't be able to qualify for a full-ride scholarship and most won't be able to completely pay for their degree just by working on the side. But most students can qualify for *some* scholarship money and most can earn *some* income on the side. Others can get help from mom and dad or grandparents. Still, others will have a working spouse who can help supplement or maybe even carry the entire weight of the household income themselves. There really are an infinite number of combinations. Every student will have their own areas of strength. The key is to leverage those strengths and combine sources to get the most out of them.

When it comes to paying for higher education, there are essentially four sources available to those who wish to avoid student debt: savings, money contributed from parents or grandparents, scholarships, and work while in school.

#6- Apply for All Available Scholarships

One of the best kept secrets about scholarships is their wide availability. During the 2014-15 school year, about two-thirds of undergraduate students received aid in the form of grants or scholarships.[37] Even at the graduate and professional school level, a majority of students receive some form of scholarship or grant. In fact, during 2011-12, 59.6 percent of graduate students received some form of aid other than loans.[38] Many students mistakenly assume that scholarships and grants are available for only a select few. This is not true in the least! If you can qualify for admittance to college or graduate school, you have a very good chance of qualifying for some scholarship or grant money.

I do need to caution you to be on your guard, however. Many colleges and universities like to brag about how much financial aid their students receive. *Financial aid* is another one of those terms which has fallen subject to academic manipulation. Often these words are used to describe not only scholarships and grants, which do not have to be paid back, but also various forms of loans. Aid that lands the student in debt is not aid at all. Be wary of this.

Depending on your particular school and area of study, there are a vast array of scholarships available from a wide variety of sources. Many schools offer institutional merit scholarships which are based on the student's academic accomplishments. Others consider factors like diversity or financial need. Government entities, non-profits, and private organizations also offer many scholarships. These may be based on diversity, civic involvement, academic achievement, need, or simply an essay contest. Several websites exist to connect students with available scholarships, and that is a good thing, because billions of dollars in available scholarship moneys go unclaimed each year.[39] So go out and get some! The best strategy is to apply for as many available scholarships as possible. You might get turned down for most, but just a few can make an enormous difference.

The Importance of Entrance Exam Scores

For both college and graduate school, the biggest factor I have observed that impacts qualification for institutional scholarships is entrance exam score. For college, this means ACT or SAT and PSAT scores. For graduate or professional school, it may mean GMAT, GRE, MCAT, LSAT, or any of the many other flavors of alphabet soup. In my observation I have found these scores to weigh substantially more heavily than GPA. The good news about this revelation is the fact that test scores can be greatly improved over a much shorter timespan than GPA. An entire industry has developed around the concept of helping prospective students improve scores on standardized entrance exams. Books, classes, and online courses exist to aid any student who is willing to put in the time. Collegeprepgenius.com is an excellent resource for students who are interested in increasing their test scores and gaining more scholarships.

If I had to go back and re-enter college or law school, the one thing I would spend the most time on is entrance exam prep. I was fortunate in high school to have a mom who encouraged me to take several practice ACTs and even attend a brief ACT prep class. As a result, I did well on the test and garnered a generous scholarship award. In preparation for the LSAT (Law School Admission Test), I spent many hours working through practice tests and practice questions on my own. I also took advantage of a simulated LSAT offered for free at a local university. Ultimately, I was pleased with my results based on the time I had invested, but I realize now that more time spent preparing may have translated into even more scholarship money. In terms of dollars per hour, entrance exam prep was by far my most profitable investment toward a debt-free education. I estimate that for the LSAT I invested approximately 80 hours in study and practice exams. Over the course of three years in law school, I received a total of $45,000 in scholarships. This translates to an hourly wage of $562.50. Even the best part-time job can't touch that hourly rate.

What You Can Do with a 2.0 GPA

One of my friends in law school was a girl from out of state named Christina. Through conversation, I found out that she had received a massive scholarship that covered most of her tuition. What was shocking is that while she was obviously an intelligent girl, she admitted that she had really goofed around during college and graduated with only about a 2.0 GPA. So how did this girl, who barely passed most of her college classes (and even failed some), end up with a substantial scholarship at a top 100 law school? Answer: she had a phenomenal LSAT score. Every school applies different standards and weights to undergraduate GPA and entrance exam scores, but Christina's story illustrates just how much test scores can influence a student's potential scholarship award. Whether they admit it or not, undergraduate, graduate, and professional schools rely heavily on test scores in awarding scholarships. Very few people can score in the top percentile of entrance exams scores, but everyone can study for, take, and retake these tests, thus increasing *their* score. And merely a few points can mean thousands of dollars. Just ask Christina. By the way, despite her abysmal GPA in college, she is now a highly successful attorney who travels all over the U.S. on her firm's dime.

#7- Work More Than You Think You Should

In this day and age, the idea of working through school can appear a bit outdated. On the university campus, it has become fashionable to nix the working and simply tack on a few more thousand dollars to the student loan tab. Many believe that working through school is a strategy more appropriate for Abraham Lincoln than for the enlightened collegiate scholars of today. If this is your view, you should change it. Let me assure you that working through school—at all levels—is just as viable today as it was when Honest Abe was swinging an axe. And it may be even more valuable.

The benefits of working while in school are numerous, and I hope to adequately outline them in this section.

Many students and parents are concerned that working during school will distract the students from their studies. What's interesting, however, is the fact that those college students who work a reasonable amount of time during the semester actually end up with *better* grades than their non-working counterparts.[40] I think the reasons for this are simple: working forces the student to prioritize their time, become more disciplined, and make better use of every available minute.

Some students don't think they can work enough during school or earn at a rate high enough to make working worthwhile. But if you have managed to graduate high school or even college, that means you already have the skills and abilities to make far above minimum wage. Don't settle. You most likely also have the means to work a job or side hustle that allows extreme flexibility with your time. This is essential for someone pursuing a rigorous graduate or undergraduate degree. Most likely many of your professors will strongly discourage working during the semester, but they aren't the ones who will ultimately be saddled with the loans, are they? If you read the first half of this book, I shouldn't have to convince you of the value of paying for school as you go. Now the question is merely how you will make it happen. Work can be a substantial factor in that equation.

Work: at the Undergraduate Level

At the undergraduate level, there is simply no reason to ever consider borrowing because the sheer opportunities to work are so plentiful. A full-time college student is in class for 15 hours per week. That's three hours per day. Even if the student spends another 15 hours each week studying (get real, they don't), that still leaves at least another 20-40 hours per week to make money. Even at minimum wage, that level of work will more than enable the student to pay for tuition at the average state school. And this is not to mention opportunities like summer break when work levels can (and probably should) easily exceed 40 hours per week. The bottom line is that the typical college schedule leaves plenty of time available for the student to work and pay for school.

Work: at the Graduate Level

While many people will admit that a moderate level of work during college is acceptable, I find it much more difficult to convince folks that working through *graduate or professional* school is tenable. Many believe the academic requirements are just too rigorous. This notion is bolstered by school faculty who are intent on students spending every spare moment on their studies. While I understand the concern, my personal experience and the observation of many other graduate students has convinced me that viable work opportunities exist for all students at all levels.

The graduate student should be able to work a job that is considerably more profitable than their undergraduate counterparts. In addition, graduate students also have more resources than most undergraduate students—more knowledge, more wisdom, more skills, and more connections.

Pro Tip: Forget about What Other People Think

Working like crazy during school is likely to make you stand apart from your classmates, but don't let that deter you. Being willing to stand out and be different was one of the most valuable skills I learned while getting my education. In law school it would not be entirely unusual for me to stroll into my afternoon classes wearing pants caked with grass and smelling of gasoline. The looks I often received were amusing. The best part is that I would usually be sitting next to some of my law school colleagues who had just returned from their law firm internships. One of the ritualistic practices in the law schools is to dress like a lawyer even if you aren't one yet, especially if you have an internship with a high-end law firm. This meant those students sitting next to me would often be decked out in thousand-dollar suits, complete with cufflinks and a handkerchief. Despite my blue-collar garb, I never felt insecure. Dirty jeans with a hundred bucks in the pocket beats a thousand-dollar suit and a negative net worth all day long.

Successfully paying for school probably means short bursts of highly profitable work, alternated with bursts of intense, highly productive study. Many academic calendars are perfectly designed for this. Heavy workloads at the beginning of the semester should gradually give way to heavier study loads toward the end. Breaks from school (summer, Christmas break, spring break, etc.) are massive opportunities for money-making labor.

During my college and law school summers I was often working 60 to 80-hour weeks in my lawn care business. But this gave my mind a much-needed break from the mental strains of academics. When I returned to school each August, my mind was refreshed and rejuvenated as was my bank account.

The Gig Economy (You _can_ work while in school)

Most students I meet who are planning to attend graduate or professional school are convinced that there are simply no options available for them to make money while in school. Now it is true that many of the professional schools attempt to limit the number of hours students work during the semester, and others ban students from being formally employed at all. But that still doesn't mean you can't _make money_ while in school. Whatever your school's policy on work may be, one of the beauties of living in this highly developed economy is that making money has become vastly more customizable than ever before.

This latest iteration of the American workplace has become known as the _gig economy_. The gig economy allows you to do work on your own schedule and at your own pace. It has replaced traditional "jobs" with gigs. If there is one company that personifies the gig economy, it's Uber. Uber was only in its infant stages when I was in school, or I definitely would have taken advantage of this fantastic income opportunity. Uber lets you work *when* you want and *how much* you want. That is the ideal arrangement for a student. I am not saying that *you* need to drive for Uber necessarily, but developing an income source with similar versatility will be invaluable.

A little creativity goes a long way in the gig economy. Even those schools that forbid formal employment can't stop you from operating an online business, making money blogging, building a multi-level hierarchy or getting paid to watch the neighbor's kids while you study. One of my law school friends operated hot air balloons on the weekends. I really don't care what you decide to do. My gig of choice was the All-American throwback: mowing lawns. But yours can be anything— anything that makes you money and fits within your schedule. Nontraditional income sources like Airbnb are springing up constantly. Now, work doesn't always look like "work" anymore. Don't let a school's shortsighted policy on employment relegate you to student loans. Our economy has evolved past that.

You never know what income sources may be lurking right under your nose. When my brother Clinton was in college, he was fortunate to get hooked up with a wealthy family in our community. They needed occasional childcare for their two sons. This family would pay my brother $200 per day along with a generous stipend for food and other activities. Often, he could even accomplish school work while the boys entertained themselves at their home. This is a prime example of the kind of gig that can make a college or graduate student big bucks and provide maximum flexibility.

While my friend Bryan was attending pharmacy school, he made his breaks count. During the summers he would sell fireworks at one of his uncle's firework stands. In just those few weeks, he was able to bring in about $7,500 dollars. It required long, hot days in the Alabama sun, but his massive short-term action had a big return.

The most effective strategy for working through school is simple: Find something that pays reasonably well and do a lot of it. By my best estimate, I personally mowed over 5,000 lawns during my college and law school years. The scheduling was flexible, and the return was excellent.

The Best Part-Time Job Is a Small Business

When it comes to making money for school, there is nothing better than some variation of a small business. House-sitting, dog-walking, yard-mowing, nannying, tutoring, photography, web design, code-writing and Ebay or Etsy stores are just a handful of ideas that make money but aren't considered employment in the traditional sense. These income sources allow the student immense flexibility with the potential to be extremely profitable. (I recently heard of a couple making $100,000 per year walking dogs.) The flexibility of working for yourself and on your own schedule, plus the potential for making more money per-hour, makes a small business the ideal method for many students. I know it was for me.

Design Your Own Internship

One of the best part-time jobs while you are in school is an internship within your field. Many of my colleagues in law school landed paid internships during the semester and summer. This is the sweet spot. No matter the field, the best way to learn is on the job, and if you can be making money while learning your craft that is a win/win. These jobs often pay well too. You will be wise to research well in advance how to qualify for the best internships. Many can be extremely lucrative but also have strict qualification criteria. However, even for those who can't achieve the sweet spot of a paid internship, all is not lost.

In law school, competition for paid internships is steep. With my work schedule, I knew I wouldn't have the grades to compete. I also knew I wanted to explore careers beyond law. So, I designed my own custom internship. I was interested in law, real estate, and business in general. I also needed to make good money. Therefore, I combined my extracurricular activities to fill these various needs. Running my lawn care business allowed me to learn valuable lessons about managing a small business, handling clients, accounting, and marketing. By getting my real estate license, I began learning the ins and outs of the real estate world and made money at the same time— all completely on my schedule. I didn't have a formal internship, but I was able to arrange my schedule to allow me to learn from mentors in various fields and simultaneously earn more experience and income. You can do the same.

You may be surprised to discover that the work you undertake through an internship or part-time job during school ends up revealing your area of passion and evolves into a lifelong career. You never know what a career is like until you try, and school is a great time to experiment with minimal risk. Take advantage of this opportunity. Internships are also a fantastic chance to build connections and develop relationships with employers. Lots of people I knew in college lined up jobs immediately out of school because they had built connections through an internship. Employers are much more amenable to hiring you if they have already witnessed your work ethic, are familiar with your skills, and like you as a person.

Why Millionaires Worked During School

There are practical benefits of working through school which go far beyond the immediate financial compensation.

Working during school is perhaps one of the best opportunities higher education provides for helping students prepare for the real world. During Dr. Stanley's research for *The Millionaire Next Door*, almost all millionaires stated that their school and college experiences influenced them in becoming productive adults later in life.[41] The factors they rated highest in this regard were "developing a strong work ethic," "learning to properly allocate time," and "working part-time jobs while in school."[42] Almost all millionaires reported that they had worked part-time jobs in undergraduate or graduate school. They credit this fact with much of their subsequent financial success. Why is this? Working during school forces the student to learn how to manage time and juggle multiple responsibilities at once—kind of like the real world. The value of this ability cannot be overstated. Students who attempt to focus exclusively on their studies miss out on the opportunity to develop these vital life skills. Also, let's just admit it: no student focuses exclusively on their studies. Netflix, social media, Greek life, keg parties, and other distractions are always present. Work helps eliminate the chance that these activities will hijack too much of a student's valuable time.

I recall one semester during college that really challenged me. I was taking 20 credit hours and was in the throes of mowing season. To handle my rigorous class and workload, I had to wake up early each day to study, attend class for several hours in the morning, and then work most afternoons and late into the evening. Wasting time wasn't an option. I was forced to carefully and efficiently allocate my time so that I didn't squander a moment. I credit that semester with helping to prepare me for the rigors of law school and my subsequent life in business.

I do want to caution that no student should overdo it. Everyone needs a reasonable amount of time for recreation and relaxation. But when it comes to college today, there is hardly an epidemic of students working too hard or too much. When in doubt, I say get to work.

#8- Be Willing to Wait

One of the most effective and yet underused strategies for getting through college or graduate school debt free is simply to delay. Nothing says you are required to start college right out of high school or a graduate program right out of college, so just relax. I meet so many college students who feel compelled to pursue their graduate degree immediately after college. If you can swing it, knocking out your degree as soon as possible is a great option; but there is absolutely nothing wrong with taking some time off—even significant time—and getting yourself more prepared before you start.

Would it shock you to know that the majority of first-year law and medical students are several years removed from college? My entering law school class had an age range of 20 to 67 with a median age of 25. You read that correctly. One of my fellow students was 67 years old and just beginning his legal education. Half of the class was over 25. It's ok if you don't start as a 22-year-old.

Young people today feel tremendous pressure to start and complete school as quickly as possible. I want to do away with any stigma attached to waiting to pursue a degree. Waiting may be the only method available for avoiding disastrous student debt loads, and there is no shame in that.

Whether you are contemplating undergraduate or graduate school, there are numerous potential benefits to waiting to pursue more education. What if, in the space of one year, you could gain admittance to a school that cost half as much as the one you have currently been admitted to? That would totally be worth it. Waiting just one more year could give you the necessary time to up your entrance exam scores, strengthen your resume and application, get accepted to a much more affordable school, and even qualify for significant scholarship money.

Refusing to wait forecloses these possibilities. What if, in the intervening period, you decide that your prospective degree program isn't for you after all? Waiting tests commitment. If you aren't willing to consider waiting even a year or two, there is a good chance you are being rash.

The Benefits of Starting Later

If you are starting college later than the norm or going back to school for a second try, you possess some real advantages. It may not feel like it, but your advanced age affords you a leg up on the average student. You are (or should be) more responsible and more mature. Hopefully, that also means you have more wisdom and a better ability to concentrate on the task at hand. Additionally, you have a compelling reason to be in school. You aren't just there to have a good time. You are there to accomplish something. Being an adult and pursuing more education means that you are ready to focus. If you have a spouse or kids, then you possess an even more noble reason for being in the classroom. It's not just about you anymore. Use that to your advantage. Most younger students don't have those profound motivations.

Nathan's 10-Year Plan

My friend Nathan (the one I referenced earlier) is a dentist and a very successful one, but he didn't start dental school until he was 32 years of age—a decade after graduating from college. During the intervening years, Nathan put together a successful career in several sales positions. When he finally decided to enter school to become a dentist, he had already purchased a home and established himself financially. Thanks to his hard work in the years after college, he was able to pay for dental school without loans. He will also tell you he was more mature, and being married with a child, had more incentives to work hard than if he had started dental school as a 22-year-old, fresh college graduate. He used the money he had saved from his sales career after undergrad, income from his working wife, and a frugal lifestyle during dental school to graduate and become a debt-free dentist. Shortly after graduation, he was in a position to purchase his own practice. In summary, Nathan waited to attend school until his 30s, which would have seemingly put him well behind those bright young students who jumped into dental school immediately out of college. But since Nathan had managed to pay for dental school without debt, he was able to acquire his own practice and reach a level of success much more quickly than his peers—even those who began with a decade head start on him.

Presidential Patience

Nathan isn't alone. In fact, he is in pretty good company. Some of America's most successful people went back to school as adults after spending extended time in the real world. Don't believe me? Let's look at some examples. President Barack Obama graduated from college in 1983. As you probably know, he would eventually go on to graduate from Harvard Law School with an impressive resume as the first black editor of the *Harvard Law Review*. However, after college Obama didn't immediately attend law school. Instead, he chose to enter the working world for several years. In fact, he would not begin at Harvard until the fall of 1988, at the ripe old age of 27. By this time, he was married and better prepared to focus on the rigorous Harvard curriculum. This strategy appears to have worked out for him.

Perhaps you find yourself on the opposite side of the political aisle from Mr. Obama and bristle at the notion of being compared to him. Very well. His predecessor, George W. Bush, was also a late bloomer when it came to graduate school. Like Obama, Bush waited five years after receiving his undergraduate degree to return to the halls of academia. Although Bush's questionable use of the English language and laid-back demeanor have been the object of much humor, he holds an MBA from the prestigious Harvard Business School, obtained after a half-decade long reprieve from education.

The point is this: taking a break between college and graduate school is not unusual. It's commonplace. And doing so has been the path to lofty success for a great many people. If you don't have the money to go right now, that's ok. Take the time to get financially prepared and then go. You will likely find that age is an asset, not a hindrance, in the quest for academic progress.

You don't have to start college at a four-year institution immediately out of high school either. Robert Lutz, former president and chairman of Chrysler Corporation, was 22 when he finally graduated from *high school*. It took him seven more years to graduate from college with a bachelor's degree. Later, well into his 30s, he even went on to earn an MBA.[43] Thousands who took a faster educational path ended up working under him as the head of one of the world's largest automobile manufacturers. For Lutz, as for many, the slow path to a degree was the fast track to mega-success.

The Incredible Value of Part-Time Programs

I am shocked at the number of students who intend to acquire more education but only consider full-time programs of study. It's as if they are unaware that part-time degree plans exist. These programs are designed to allow the student to hold down a full-time job and still earn a degree. What's most amazing is the fact that many part-time programs don't take much longer to complete than the full-time track. In many law schools, for instance, the full-time law degree track is a three-year program, while the part-time track is only five years. This is a fantastic option for multiple reasons. The greatest benefit is obviously the availability of the student to work more while in school. That's invaluable. However, the stretched-out nature of the program also means that tuition costs will be stretched out as well. In other words, you will have more time to get the money together to pay cash. No one who has a part-time degree track available to them needs to borrow for school. Remember, quicker is not always better.

Your Grades Don't Matter

One of the major objections I encounter to the idea of working during school is the argument that if the student works, their grades will suffer. I want to clue you in on a really important tip for college or graduate school which most academics would adamantly deny: YOUR GRADES DO NOT MATTER. I mean that. I know your parents told you growing up how important it was to work hard in school and get good grades. So did mine. They meant well but they were wrong—at least about most letter grades. Outside of a few exceptions, the primary concern anyone should have about grades is whether or not they're passing. The only reason grades in high school matter is for getting into college. The only reason college grades matter is for getting into graduate school. If you don't plan to take your schooling beyond the level of an undergraduate degree, then your college grades don't matter. Graduate school grades pretty much just don't matter. Very few people ever ask or care what GPA you carried as long as you graduate.

Now don't misunderstand me, I did not say that *learning* doesn't matter or that *knowledge* doesn't matter. I said *grades* don't matter. There were plenty of occasions in both college and law school when I crammed the information for a test into my brain just fast enough to pass the exam and then forget it all within a week. I may have received a high letter grade but didn't retain valuable knowledge. Was that the proper objective? I would have been better served to have received a C but made certain that I remembered what was most important. It wasn't the grade that mattered. It was the knowledge. You want to learn the material as well as possible and be certain to retain the information that will be useful in the future. But a grade point average is just a number. There is little use in stressing over the difference between a 3.2 and 3.3. In general, I see students (and parents) placing far too much emphasis on this extremely relative measure of academic success.

Still not convinced? What kind of grades do you think most millionaires garnered in college? Were they all 4.0's? Did they graduate Summa Cum Laude? For the most part, no. *The average American millionaire carried a 2.9 GPA through college.*[44] That means most millionaires were well accustomed to collecting B's and even C's at the end of the semester. This doesn't mean they didn't learn anything in school. It just means that they weren't fanatical about grades. Most also made it a priority to develop interpersonal skills, foster relationships, and build practical experience outside the classroom.

It's important to remember that almost all

millionaires (90%) *did graduate from college.*[45] So when it comes to millionaire status, a college degree is nearly a prerequisite. However, it is equally important to remember that most of these economic successes did not place an undue emphasis on overall GPA. Their foremost intention was to collect the degree and useful knowledge in the most efficient manner possible. Grades were not their primary concern.

In college many required classes contain extremely relevant and useful material, while others do not. Even at the professional and graduate school level, there are some classes that really matter. Others don't. Your job is to figure out how to allocate your resources accordingly. If you believe you will use the knowledge in the future, learn the material thoroughly. If you are sure you won't, do what it takes to pass the class and achieve a sufficient grade. To do more would be wasteful.

I finished my first undergraduate semester with a 4.0 GPA. I was extremely proud of myself. I spent enormous amounts of time studying and significant energy stressing. I even dropped my French class toward the end of the semester because I was worried I might only receive a B—a grade which would tarnish my perfect record. Sometime during my second semester, I realized that all this stress and time was stealing from my other pursuits. So, I lightened up on the grades. I still studied hard, but I also took more time to work and build relationships. My quality of life was better, I accomplished more, and I still managed to graduate with a respectable 3.67 GPA.

I maintained this philosophy in law school. There, because I was working so much, my grades did suffer at times. However, I am happy to report that despite my low

GPA, I did graduate with honors. The honors were: I received a piece of paper and I got to leave the school. Those were the honors that mattered to me. In the time I have been practicing law, no client has ever asked what my GPA was.

It may seem I am being slightly dramatic about grades. While I will stick to my guns on the assertion that, after graduation, no one cares about your GPA, there are a few occasions where grades do matter. One, as I mentioned earlier, is for the purposes of taking the next step in your education. Grades in college matter principally for admission and possible qualification for scholarship money for graduate school. Good grades also help in qualifying for paid internships, institutional scholarships, or fellowships.

In law school, grades during the first semester were a big deal for some, because the students who received the highest grades during that term were selected to interview with the top firms for summer internships. This didn't matter to me, because I was planning to work outside of law during the summer anyway. However, for those who wanted a crack at interning for certain law firms, grades were relevant.

Some schools will hand out scholarships to select upper-class students based on their performance. This is one other instance in which grades may matter. However, I will caution that these scholarships are rare and generally very small. I wouldn't lose much sleep hoping to qualify for one. Your time would probably be better spent working a side job for which you know you will get paid. I know mine was.

If you are still skeptical about how concerned you

should be about your GPA, I have an assignment for you. Find someone who has been out of school for a while and still has a considerable student loan balance. (That shouldn't be difficult.) Ask them how many grade points they would trade from their GPA for each $10,000 in debt. Their answers will tell you all you need to know.

Proof It Can Be Done:
Other People Who Have Done It

As I've said before, for most students, paying for college or graduate school is a combination of things: scholarship money, savings, help from mom and dad, part-time work and maybe a summer job. If you can scrape together a little money from several of these sources, the task of paying cash for school becomes achievable. However, depending on the particular degree you are seeking, things like the prospects of work during school and cost of tuition can vary dramatically. Some higher-level graduate degrees can seem nearly impossible to pay for without debt. In the coming section, I will highlight some people that I know who have managed to attain their graduate and professional degrees with no debt whatsoever. You may not elect to pursue the exact strategy which any of these individuals chose to employ, but the fact that they were able to pay for school with cash is evidence that it can be done, and you can do it too.

The Fellowship

Many families have a perfect kid—the sibling that all the other siblings are measured by and continually come up short against. In my family that was my oldest brother, Benjamin. As the first child, he did my other brother, sister, and I a favor and eliminated any possibility that we would be able to match his achievements by setting the academic bar unreachably high. There was never any pressure because we knew none of us were going to be as smart as he was. However, the one chink in his armor is the fact that he *didn't* get a perfect score on the ACT. He received only 35 out of the available 36 points. I like to hold that over his head. Benjamin is a math guy, and when we would go on family vacations, he would bring along Calculus and Trigonometry books just for fun. I know, a total freak. It's worked out for him though. Today, he is an actuary for one of the largest insurance companies in the nation. (If you don't know what an actuary is, it's a nerd who gets paid an obscene salary to tabulate statistics about how quickly you and I are going to die.) Benjamin isn't just good at math—he's brilliant at life. He even figured out a way to get the university to pay *him* for his graduate degrees, rather than the other way around. Maybe I should have brought some math books on vacation.

The method my brother employed to get his education paid for is known as a *fellowship*. Not everyone can qualify for this type of arrangement, but for those who can, it is a sweet deal. A fellowship involves the graduate student agreeing to work for the university by doing research or acting as a teaching assistant (TA). While my brother was pursuing both his master's and doctorate degree in statistics at the University of Kentucky, he served as a TA for some undergraduate classes. In exchange for his services, the university covered the cost of both his degrees and even paid him a monthly stipend for living expenses. Not too shabby.

For many graduate programs, the fellowship is the jackpot. Qualify for one, and your path to a debt-free degree is paved in gold. If you are a prospective graduate student, I would suggest thoroughly researching the possibility of applying for a fellowship in your field. The good news is you don't have to be a genius nerd like my brother to qualify for most fellowships or teaching assistantships. You will, however, need a solid record of academic performance and a resume chock-full of relevant experience.

Tuition Remission

My wife Meg, who is also brilliant, devised a different but equally effective strategy for paying for her MBA (Master of Business Administration) degree. As I mentioned earlier, Meg and I met in college when I was a freshman and she was junior. That's right, we have a cougar on our hands, ladies and gentlemen. Her advanced age (in relation to mine) is something I rarely let her forget.

Meg graduated two years before me and needed to kill time while she was waiting on me to finish school. She also apparently thought the prospects for my financial success were somewhat shaky and, if we were going to be together, one of us would need a stable income. So she decided to pursue an MBA. She's smart and tight with her money so she didn't want to pay too much or go into debt. She also required an income to live on while she was taking classes. Immediately after college graduation, she moved back to her hometown in Tennessee, which is also home to a thriving mid-major university. Meg applied for and was granted a job in the admissions office of that university's newly-built medical school. The pay was modest, commensurate with the salary of most jobs for fresh college grads, but the position included one spectacular benefit: *tuition remission.*

Tuition remission is a benefit available to many full-time employees of universities which allows the employees, their spouses, and children to waive the tuition for courses taken at that university. In other words, while Meg was working for the university full time, she was able to take her MBA classes at night, completely free of charge. In fact, because she is so tight, Meg was able to knock out her MBA, pay for her living expenses, and even put some money in the bank, all thanks to the tuition remission program and her modest salary. If you can find an arrangement like this, you've struck the motherload.

If some variation of this program is available to you, I recommend that you look into it seriously. Research carefully and make certain that the terms of the program fit with your life circumstances and expectations for the near future. If so, this possibility is a slam dunk for a debt-free education.

Employer-Paid Tuition

Colleges are not the only entities that offer tuition benefits for their employees. More and more companies are figuring out that it is advantageous to have well-educated team members who are not drowning in debt. I have many friends who have received from their employers thousands of dollars in aid toward their schooling. From industrial manufacturing to the medical field, companies are anxious to help their employees become better at their jobs.

You don't necessarily have to already be employed

to receive this benefit, either. If you have selected the field in which you want to work, it is a good idea to contact companies in that field to see if any are willing to pay for your training in exchange for your commitment to work for them after graduation. This is a clever recruitment tool for the company and an added incentive for the prospective employee. It may require additional legwork, and you may have to think outside the box, but the ROI of this type of arrangement could be substantial.

The Military

My buddy Aaron is one bad dude. He played football for the University of West Virginia and then survived Army Ranger School. For those of you unfamiliar with this program, it is the gauntlet experience to which the U.S. Army subjects its top cadets, challenging their physical and mental ability to survive in the wild for 61 days, through hunger and sleep deprivation. The program qualifications are extremely stringent, and yet, only about 50% of those who do qualify, manage to complete it. I told you he was a bad dude. Now, he is also a lawyer.

I met Aaron in my Constitutional Law class at U of L. By that time, he was married with three kids. We sat in the back row and caused trouble like two punks in a high school classroom.

As I got to know Aaron, I found out he was going through law school without debt just like me. When I asked him how, he said the Army was paying for it. Aaron was committed to working for the Army for a certain number of hours while in school and for a period of years afterward. In exchange, the Army was picking up the tab for his law school tuition and providing a stipend for his family to live on for several years. That is a tremendous debt-free deal!

I remember visiting Aaron at his home during one of the semester breaks. I was shocked to witness what a fantastic situation his family was in. They were living in a wonderful home in suburban Louisville. He was able to attend law school full time and still had plenty of time to spend with his kids and wife. What was even more amazing was the fact that they would not have to worry about paying back hundreds of thousands of dollars in loans when he got out of school. Additionally, he already had a job lined up immediately after graduation.

I understand that the military option is not for everyone. This route poses costs and risks that other pathways do not. However, no one can deny its extraordinary benefits. As far as sure-fire, debt-free strategies go, the military is one of the most widely available options. You just have to be willing to serve. The required commitment is considerable, but the payoff is gargantuan. These types of arrangements are available in all branches of the Armed Forces for most every degree level, from an associate degree to a Doctor of Medicine. It's a great way to serve your country and to let your country serve you.

Examples Are Everywhere

The examples above hardly do justice to the myriad of methods available for paying cash for school. They are just a sample. If 70% of students are borrowing for college, that means 30% aren't. A debt-free education is uncommon, but it isn't impossible. Draw inspiration from those who have already accomplished this feat.

Be Different

You *can* go to school without loans. The people at the schools will tell you it can't be done. The politicians, the media, and most of your friends will tell you it can't be done. But far too many people have proven and continue to prove that it *can* be done. Choosing to pay cash for school is a decision to be different. I think it is worth revisiting the fact that 76% of millionaires reported that *learning to think differently than the crowd* while they were in their formative years was an important influence in becoming productive adults later in life.[46] The willingness to stand out and be different has inherent value. It's a necessity for getting through school without loans and an incredibly valuable asset during the remainder of life. If you remember just one thing from this section or this book, I hope you will remember this: Being debt free is uncommon, but so is being successful. Don't let the fear of being different prevent you from achieving success. Choosing not to conform might just be the most powerful decision you can ever make.

Thanks for Reading

Thank you for taking the time to read this book. I hope I've ruffled your feathers at times, because if I haven't, I haven't done my job. If you have made it this far, that hopefully means you have found something useful in these pages. If you have, the highest compliment you can pay me as an author is to go and implement this information in your own life and to tell others about this message.

It's a difficult task to change cultural norms, but when those norms are faulty and harmful, they must be changed. I hope you will join me in seeking to modify how this culture approaches higher education. If you have a degree to pursue, that change will start with you.

Now you know how I did it. Now you know how others have done it. And now I know that *you* will do it, because you know it's worth it.

Acknowledgements

To Mom—I may not have any student debt, but as your student I will always be indebted to you. You taught me how to read, to write, to think, and to work. You are in a tie as the wisest woman I have ever known. Thanks for consistently investing in me—even when it looked like my stock was dropping. You and Dad have truly blessed me with gifts infinitely more valuable than money. I love you.

To my writing buddy, Bryan Taylor—You are the divinely appointed catalyst that finally got me moving. Without you, I firmly believe I would never have completed this project. Thanks for the accountability, encouragement, and all the word count texts. If I ever sell half the books that you do, I'll be doing alright.

To Tucker and Parker—You guys make debt-free college look easy. Someone must have taught you how to work. Thanks for your insights and contributions to this book. You'll both be millionaires by 30.

To the mom of Tucker and Parker—Thanks for taking enormous amounts of time to contribute to this book. You did more than I ever could have imagined, and I will never be able to repay you.

To Benjamin—Somehow you know exactly what kind of encouragement I need—a kind word or a kick in the pants. You use them both expertly as only an older brother could. Thanks for living a life worth emulating and making time to share your interests with me.

To Michael Blue—Thank you for giving this wannabe author the time of day. Your encouragement on this project was an indispensable confirmation.

And finally, to Meg—you loved me as a broke college kid, a law school failure, and even now. For some reason you believe in me, even when I give up on myself. Thank you for inspiring me every day. I know you married me for my youth and for my money. The youth is running out, so I hope the money comes soon. You're the wisest girl I know, and with you I have no lack of gain.

I like you, you know.

Notes

[1] U.S. Student Loan Debt Statistics for 2018. (n.d.). Retrieved March 12, 2018, from https://studentloanhero.com/student-loan-debt-statistics/

[2] Stanley, Thomas J. (2000). *The Millionaire Mind.* Kansas City, MO: Andrews McMeel Publishing.

[3] The Institute for College Access and Success. (n.d.). Retrieved March 6, 2018 from https://ticas.org/fact-sheets-about-student-debt-and-financial-aid

[4] Delisle, J., Phillips, van der Linde, R. (2014). The Graduate Student Debt Review: The State of Graduate Student Borrowing. Retrieved March 6, 2018, from https://static.newamerica.org/attachments/750-the-graduate-student-debt-review/GradStudentDebtReview-Delisle-Final.pdf

[5] Delisle, J., Phillips, van der Linde, R. (2014). The Graduate Student Debt Review: The State of Graduate Student Borrowing. Retrieved March 6, 2018, from https://static.newamerica.org/attachments/750-the-graduate-student-debt-review/GradStudentDebtReview-Delisle-Final.pdf

[6]National Center for Education Statistics. (n.d.). Percentage distribution of graduate students who received financial aid by composition of aid, by selected enrollment and student characteristics: 1995–96, 1999–2000, 2003–04, 2007–08, and 2011–12. Retrieved March 6, 2018, from https://nces.ed.gov/datalab/tableslibrary/viewtable.aspx?tableid=9829

[7] College Board. (n.d.). Answers to Your Frequently Asked Questions about Financial Aid. Retrieved March 6, 2018, from https://bigfuture.collegeboard.org/pay-for-college/financial-aid-101/financial-aid-faqs

[8] Elvery, Joel. (2018). Is there a student loan crisis? Not in payments. Retrieved March 6, 2018, from https://clevelandfed.org/newsroom-and-events/publications/forefront/ff-v7n02/ff-20160516-v7n0204-is-there-a-student-loan-crisis.aspx

[9] Bidwell, Allie. (2014). Student Loans Expectations: Myth vs. Reality. Retrieved March 6, 2018, from http://www.usnews.com/news/blogs/data-mine/2014/10/07/student-loan-expectations-myth-vs-reality

[10] Stanley, Thomas J. (2000). *The Millionaire Mind.* Kansas City, MO: Andrews McMeel Publishing.

[11] Stanley, Thomas J. and Danko, William D. (1996). *The Millionaire Next Door.* Marietta, GA: Longstreet Press, Inc.

[12] Stanley, Thomas J. (2000). *The Millionaire Mind.* Kansas City, MO: Andrews McMeel Publishing.

[13] Stanley, Thomas J. and Danko, William D. (1996). *The Millionaire Next Door.* Marietta, GA: Longstreet Press, Inc.

[14] Twenge, J.M. (2014). *Generation Me: Why Today's Young Americans Are More Confident, Assertive, Entitled, and More Miserable Than Ever Before.* New York: Simon & Schuster.

[15] Twenge, J.M. (2014). *Generation Me: Why Today's Young Americans Are More Confident, Assertive, Entitled, and More Miserable Than Ever Before.* New York: Simon & Schuster

[16] Wile, Rob. (2015, April 13). It took Marco Rubio 16 years and a book deal to pay off his student loans. Retrieved March 6, 2018, from https://splinternews.com/it-took-marco-rubio-16-years-and-a-book-deal-to-pay-off-1793847061

[17] Bidwell, Allie. (2014). Student Loans Expectations: Myth vs. Reality. Retrieved March 6, 2018, from http://www.usnews.com/news/blogs/data-mine/2014/10/07/student-loan-expectations-myth-vs-reality

[18] Center for Disease Control and Prevention. (2017, September). Youth and Tobacco Use. Retrieved March 6, 2018, from https://www.cdc.gov/tobacco/data_statistics/fact_sheets/youth_data/tobacco_use/

[19] Carlozo, Lou. (2012). Why College Students Stop Short of a Degree. Reuters. Retrieved March 7, 2018, from http://www.reuters.com/article/us-attn-andrea-education-dropouts-idUSBRE82Q0Y120120327

[20] Okahana, Hironao. (2017). Master's Completion Project. Council of Graduate Schools. Retrieved March 7, 2018, from http://cgsnet.org/masters-completion-project

[21] Garrison, G., Mikesell, C. &, Matthew, D. (2007, April). Analysis in Brief/Association of American Medical Colleges,7. Retrieved March 6, 2018, from https://www.aamc.org/download/379220/data/may2014aib-

[22] Kentucky Office of Bar Admissions. (n.d.). Retrieved March 6, 2018, from http://www.kyoba.org/

[23] Twenge, J.M. (2014). *Generation Me: Why Today's Young Americans Are More Confident, Assertive, Entitled, and More Miserable Than Ever Before.* New York: Simon & Schuster.

[24] Kristof, Kathy. (2013, September 10). $1 million mistake: Becoming a Doctor. MoneyWatch. Retrieved March 6, 2018, from http://www.cbsnews.com/news/1-million-mistake-becoming-a-doctor/

[25] Twenge, J.M. (2014). *Generation Me: Why Today's Young Americans Are More Confident, Assertive, Entitled, and More Miserable Than Ever Before.* New York: Simon & Schuster.

[26] Banks, Kerry. (2010). *Baseball's Top 100: The Game's Greatest Records.* Vancouver, BC: Greystone Books.

[27] Bureau of Labor Statistics. (2017, August 24). Number of Jobs, Labor Market Experience, and Earnings Growth Among Americans at 50: Results from a Longitudinal Survey. News Release. Retrieved March 6, 2018, from https://www.bls.gov/news.release/pdf/nlsoy.pdf

[28] Plumer, Brad. (2013, May 20). Only 27 Percent of College Grads Have a Job Related to Their Major. The Washington Post. Retrieved March 7, 2018, from https://www.washingtonpost.com/news/wonk/wp/2013/05/20/ only-27-percent-of-college-grads-have-a-job-related-to-their-major/?utm_term=.2d601dff969f

[29] Meister, Jeanne. The Future of Work: Job Hopping is the 'New Normal' for Millennials. Forbes. Retrieved March 6, 2018, from http://www.forbes.com/sites/jeannemeister/2012/08/14/the-future-of-work-job-hopping-is-the-new-normal-for-millennials/#4b459b86322

[30] Mataconis, Doug. (2013, May 20). Most College Graduates Have Jobs Unrelated to their Major. Outside the Beltway. Retrieved March 6, 2018, from http://www.outsidethebeltway.com/most-college-graduates-have-jobs-unrelated-to-their-major/

[31] Scholarship America. (2011, October 27). Uncover the Real Costs of Public and Private Colleges. U.S. News and World Report. Retrieved March 6, 2018, from https://www.usnews.com/education/blogs/the-scholarship-coach/2011/10/27/uncover-the-real-costs-of-public-and-private-colleges

[32] George Graduate School of Education and Human Development. (n.d.). In-state vs. Out-of-State Tuition. Retrieved March 6, 2018, from https://www.heath.gwu.edu/state-vs-out-state-tuition

[33] Stanley, Thomas J. (2000). *The Millionaire Mind.* Kansas City, MO: Andrews McMeel Publishing.

[34] Stanley, Thomas J. (2000). *The Millionaire Mind.* Kansas City, MO: Andrews McMeel Publishing.

[35] Brandeis School of Law website. Retrieved March 7, 2018, from http://louisville.edu/law/

[36] Law School Transparency website. Retrieved March 7, 2018, from https://www.lstreports.com/schools/louisville/

[37] College Board. (n.d.). Financial Aid: Frequently Asked Questions. Retrieved March 7, 2018, from https://bigfuture.collegeboard.org/pay-for-college/financial-aid-101/financial-aid-faqs

[38] National Center for Education Statistics. (n.d.). Percentage distribution of graduate students who received financial aid by composition of aid, by selected enrollment and student characteristics: 1995–96, 1999–2000, 2003–04, 2007–08, and 2011–12. Retrieved March 6, 2018, from https://nces.ed.gov/datalab/tableslibrary/viewtable.aspx?tableid=9829

[39] Hoyt, Elizabeth. (2015, January 20). Over $2.9 Billion Free College Money Unclaimed by Students – Why? Fastweb. Retrieved March 7, 2018, from https://www.fastweb.com/financial-aid/articles/over-2-point-nine-billion-in-free-college-money-unclaimed-by-students-why

[40] National Center for Education Statistics. (n.d.). Percentage distribution of graduate students who received financial aid by composition of aid, by selected enrollment and student

characteristics: 1995–96, 1999–2000, 2003–04, 2007–08, and 2011–12. Retrieved March 6, 2018, from https://nces.ed.gov/datalab/tableslibrary/viewtable.aspx?tableid=9829

[41] Stanley, Thomas J. (2000). *The Millionaire Mind.* Kansas City, MO: Andrews McMeel Publishing.

[42] Stanley, Thomas J. (2000). *The Millionaire Mind.* Kansas City, MO: Andrews McMeel Publishing.

[43] Stanley, Thomas J. (2000). *The Millionaire Mind.* Kansas City, MO: Andrews McMeel Publishing.

[44] Stanley, Thomas J. (2000). *The Millionaire Mind.* Kansas City, MO: Andrews McMeel Publishing.

[45] Stanley, Thomas J. (2000). *The Millionaire Mind.* Kansas City, MO: Andrews McMeel Publishing.

[46] Stanley, Thomas J. (2000). *The Millionaire Mind.* Kansas City, MO: Andrews McMeel Publishing.

91454642R00108

Made in the USA
Columbia, SC
16 March 2018